ROUTLEDGE LIBRARY EDITIONS:
CURRICULUM

Volume 27

CURRICULUM STUDIES

CURRICULUM STUDIES
An Introductory Annotated Bibliography

Edited by
COLIN RICHARDS

LONDON AND NEW YORK

First edition published in 1978
Second edition published in 1984 by Falmer

This edition first published in 2019
by Routledge
2 Park Square, Milton Park, Abingdon, Oxon OX14 4RN

and by Routledge
711 Third Avenue, New York, NY 10017

Routledge is an imprint of the Taylor & Francis Group, an informa business

© 1984 Colin Richards, editorial matter

All rights reserved. No part of this book may be reprinted or reproduced or utilised in any form or by any electronic, mechanical, or other means, now known or hereafter invented, including photocopying and recording, or in any information storage or retrieval system, without permission in writing from the publishers.

Trademark notice: Product or corporate names may be trademarks or registered trademarks, and are used only for identification and explanation without intent to infringe.

British Library Cataloguing in Publication Data
A catalogue record for this book is available from the British Library

ISBN: 978-1-138-31956-1 (Set)
ISBN: 978-0-429-45387-8 (Set) (ebk)
ISBN: 978-1-138-31900-4 (Volume 27) (hbk)
ISBN: 978-1-138-32191-5 (Volume 27) (pbk)
ISBN: 978-0-429-45414-1 (Volume 27) (ebk)

Publisher's Note
The publisher has gone to great lengths to ensure the quality of this reprint but points out that some imperfections in the original copies may be apparent.

Disclaimer
The publisher has made every effort to trace copyright holders and would welcome correspondence from those they have been unable to trace.

CURRICULUM STUDIES

An Introductory Annotated Bibliography

compiled by
COLIN RICHARDS

*Formerly of
University of Leicester*

Second edition

 The Falmer Press

*A member of the
Taylor & Francis Group
London and New York*

© Editorial matter copyright Colin Richards 1984. All rights reserved. No part of this publication may be reproduced, stored in a retrieval system, or transmitted, in any form or by any means, electronic, mechanical, photocopying, recording or otherwise, without the prior permission in writing from the Publisher.

Second Edition published 1984

ISBN Paper only 0 905273 44 3

Typeset in 9/10 and 11/12 Plantin by
Imago Publishing Ltd, Thame, Oxon

Printed and bound by Taylor and Francis (Printers) Ltd
Basingstoke for

The Falmer Press
(*A member of the Taylor and Francis Group*)
Falmer House
Barcombe, Lewes
Sussex BN8 5DL
England

Contents

		Page
	Introduction	vi
1	**Curriculum Studies**	1
	Introductory texts	1
	More advanced texts	3
	General readers and conference papers	3
	Other sources	6
2	**The Socio-cultural Context**	8
	Sociology of the curriculum	8
	Culture and the curriculum	16
3	**Curriculum History** (compiled by David Hamilton)	20
4	**Curriculum Agents and Agencies**	23
	National	23
	Local	25
5	**Curriculum Design**	28
	General	28
	Objectives-based designs, critiques and alternatives	32
	Psychology and curriculum design	36
6	**Curriculum Development**	38
	General	38
	Project-based development	42
	School-focussed development	44
	Curriculum dissemination, adoption and implementation	47
7	**Curriculum Management** (compiled by Ken Shaw)	52
8	**Curriculum Evaluation, Assessment and Accountability**	54
9	**Curriculum 'Theory' and Research**	67
	Curriculum 'theory'	67
	Curriculum research	72
10	**'Official' Curriculum Publications**	79
11	**Curriculum Journals**	82
12	**Addendum**	84
	Author and Editor Index	86

Introduction (to the First Edition)

Curriculum studies is a fast developing area within the field of education. It is now established as an integral part of most initial teacher-education courses and an important component of many advanced courses at advanced diploma and higher degree levels. Ten years ago it was heavily dependent on American theorizing and research, but since then a distinctive British 'tradition' has developed. Though drawing on some American material, this bibliography attempts to introduce students and teachers to the British 'tradition' which has diverged markedly (and, many would argue, fruitfully) from its transatlantic counterpart. The present bibliography is the successor to a mimeographed one first produced five years ago: the remarkable difference in their contents (especially in the proportion of American material) bears witness to the flowering of curriculum studies in the United Kingdom.

I need to stress that this bibliography is intended for those on the 'edge' of, or just 'inside', the field of curriculum studies. It is designed to help students taking BEd. and advanced diploma courses and those M.Ed. students at an early stage of their course. With such an audience in mind I have been highly (and idiosyncratically) selective: my large card file of unused entries illustrates this. It is always difficult to know just how to organise such material: in a developing area there is no consensus as to its boundaries, its internal structure, even its problems and procedures! Users wanting justification for the organisation adopted here should read *An Introduction to Curriculum Studies* (N.F.E.R., 1979) written by Philip Taylor and myself. It is also a problem whether to include appraisals alongside summaries: in the end I have decided to include them in most cases, since I feel they may add interest and a personal touch and may even incite users to react against my judgements. However, it must be stressed that these judgements are mine alone: defensible but personal.

At this point I need to acknowledge the help of three former colleagues from Worcester College of Higher Education: Derek Sharples who originally suggested the need for such a bibliography (partly, he would admit, to get me off his back!); and Dick Puttock and Dan Wicksteed who helped compile an earlier version and some of whose comments can still be traced in this published edition.

Lastly I write to invite users' reactions. There are almost certainly many important references I have neglected to include (partly through prejudice and largely through ignorance). Please let me know of these. Judging from past experience, I am sure another, very different edition of this bibliography will be required five years on.

Colin Richards
October 1978

Introduction (To the Second Edition)

A greatly enlarged second edition of the bibliography has proved to be necessary about five years on from the publication of the first edition. This is the result, partly of the continuing development of curriculum studies in the United Kingdom, partly of the interest shown in the curriculum by scholars in other areas of educational enquiry, and partly of the rapid changes in the socio-cultural context in which the curriculum is discussed, designed and transacted. This edition reflects these developments: it is almost twice as long as the previous publication; it contains new sections on curriculum history (compiled by David Hamilton), curriculum management (compiled by Ken Shaw), 'official' publications, and journals; it has greatly expanded sections on the sociology of the curriculum and on curriculum evaluation, assessment, and accountability. The book retains its British emphasis; no attempt is made to introduce readers, except indirectly, to developments in curriculum studies in North America. In one respect I have revised my original conception of the bibliography: I now believe that it can serve not only students on B.Ed. courses and advanced diploma courses but also M.Ed. students throughout their courses, though some of the reading undertaken by the latter may well go beyond my entries. As before, I would like users' reactions. A third edition is a distinct possibility — made more likely if users, once 'inside' the field, make their own contribution to the development of curriculum studies through publishing material based on their own thinking and/or research. Entries are thus invited for the 1988 edition!

Colin Richards
March 1983

ABBREVIATIONS

The following abbreviations are used in the bibliography:

B.J. Ednl. Psych.	British Journal of Educational Psychology
B.J. Ednl. Studies	British Journal of Educational Studies
B.J. Ednl. Technology	British Journal of Educational Technology
Cambridge J.Ed.	Cambridge Journal of Education
Ednl. Admin.	Educational Administration
J. Curriculum Studies	Journal of Curriculum Studies
London Ednl. R.	London Educational Review
Universities Q.,	Universities Quarterly
Phil. of Ed. Soc.Proc.	Proceedings of the Philosophy of Education Society of Great Britain
Scottish Ednl. Studies	Scottish Educational Studies

Unless otherwise stated, books are published in London.

1 Curriculum Studies

Introductory texts

1 GORDON, P. (Ed.), *The Study of the Curriculum*, Batsford Academic and Educational, 1981

   Yet another introduction and restatement of the views of the London Institute 'school' of curriculum studies (see 5). The book is divided into three sections ('Values and the Curriculum', 'Historical and Political' and 'Curriculum Planning') and each chapter has suggestions for further reading and questions for the reader to consider. Intended as a textbook and reads like one!

2 JENKINS, D. and SHIPMAN, M., *Curriculum: An Introduction*, Open Books, 1976

   A useful, though uneven, attempt to put the curriculum in socio/historical context and curriculum studies in an academic context. Curriculum studies is characterised as eclectic, unstable but potentially usable: an apt summary description of the book itself.

3 KELLY, A., *The Curriculum: Theory and Practice*, (second edition) Harper and Row, 1982

   A useful overview of thinking within the field of curriculum studies in Britain and of the influences and constraints impinging on the planning, management and evaluation of the curriculum. Re-organizes and up-dates the material in the first edition and contains a new chapter on 'The Political Context'. Attempts to reconcile 'a proper measure of external control' with 'the natural and essential evolution of the curriculum from within' the schools.

4 KERR, J. (Ed), *Changing the Curriculum*, University of London Press, 1968

   Based on a series of lectures (by Kerr, Hirst, Charlton, Taylor and Musgrove) dealing with the problem of curriculum reform and the contributions of the disciplines of education to the study of the curriculum. A valuable collection, now inevitably dated, especially the papers on curriculum reform and the contribution of sociology.

5 LAWTON, D. et al., *Theory and Practice of Curriculum Studies*, Routledge and Kegan Paul, 1978

A decidedly uneven collection of papers originally written as a series of lectures for diploma students. Exemplifies the London Institute's multi-disciplinary approach to curriculum studies with philosophical, psychological, sociological and historical contributions. More about 'theory' than about 'practice' in curriculum studies.

6 SKILBECK, M., *Basic Questions in Curriculum*, E. 203, *Curriculum Design and Development*, unit 2, Open University Press, Milton Keynes, 1976

A clearly written, genuinely introductory examination of five major questions (e.g. What shall I teach? Why shall I teach it?). Distinguishes between a problem-centred view of curriculum studies and an applied discipline view.

7 SMITH, B., STANLEY, W. and SHORES, J., *Fundamentals of Curriculum Development*, Harcourt, Brace and World, New York, 1957

A classic (and massive) American text. Introductory chapters useful for putting the school curriculum in a very broad socio/cultural context. Also useful is part three devoted to discussing basic forms of curriculum organisation — subject, activity and core.

8 TABA, H., *Curriculum Development: Theory and Practice*, Harcourt, Brace and World, New York, 1962

Another classic American text of considerable length which provides an overview of a particular style of curriculum thinking developed in the U.S.A. during the late 50s and early 60s. Though now dated and inappropriately compendious, it contains some useful chapters, especially the second part on the process of curriculum planning.

9 TAYLOR, P. and RICHARDS, C, *An Introduction to Curriculum Studies*, NFER, Windsor, 1979

An introductory synthesis attempting to provide an overall framework in which the beginning student can locate key issues and major pieces of work. Attempts to give students an initial 'sense' of the field and a 'feel' for its concerns and complexities. Contains plentiful references and suggestions for further reading.

More Advanced Texts

10   EISNER, E., *The Educational Imagination: On the Design and Evaluation of School Programs*, Collier-Macmillan, 1979

A superb book, beautifully written and full of insights into teaching, learning and the curriculum. Its main concern is to discuss the uses of artistic forms of understanding and reflection in the design and evaluation of curricula, but it raises many other issues. Written for an American readership, but English readers must not be put off by this. Its clarity, incisiveness and subtlety are best appreciated by students who have already read (endured?) the standard introductions to curriculum studies.

11   GOODLAD, J. et al., *Curriculum Inquiry: The Study of Curriculum Practice*, McGraw-Hill, New York, 1979

Provides a conceptual framework for the study of curriculum practice, aspects of which are filled out by various co-authors. The framework involves two sources of data for curriculum planning ('funded knowledge' and 'conventional wisdom'), four domains (societal, institutional, instructional and personal/experiential) in which decisions are made, and curricular transactions and interpretations. Research and case-studies illustrating aspects of the model are discussed. A sophisticated attempt to conceptualise the social, political and technical aspects of curriculum practice.

12   STENHOUSE, L., *An Introduction to Curriculum Research and Development*, Heinemann, 1975

More an introduction to Stenhouse than an introduction to curriculum studies. It's a fascinating, insightful and at times difficult text which examines the field from one particular perspective. Particularly valuable on curriculum design issues and on development from an 'insider's' perspective. Not a book for the absolute beginner but essential for those some way into the field.

General Readers and Conference Papers

13   FINCH, A. and SCRIMSHAW, P. (Eds.), *Standards, Schooling and Education*, Hodder and Stoughton/Open University Press, 1980

A useful collection of articles focusing on values in education, standards, schooling and social change, and controlling the curriculum. Contains a wide variety of educational/political perspectives, carefully marshalled by the editors who provide valuable introductions. Contains only one paper specially written for the book. A complementary reader to that edited by REEDY and WOODHEAD (18).

14 GALTON, M. (Ed.), *Curriculum Change: The Lessons of a Decade*, Leicester University Press, Leicester, 1980

A rather disappointing collection of essays examining aspects of Kerr's curriculum model a decade or so on from its original publication (see 4). The collection is loosely put together: as the editor admits, 'no attempt was made to brief each contributor except in general terms with a mandate to look both backward and forward on the curriculum scene'. Contains an interesting essay by Kelly: 'From innovation to adaptability: the changing perspective of curriculum development' and an updated defence of rational curriculum planning by HIRST: *The Logic of Curriculum Development*.

15 GOLBY, M. et al. (Eds.), *Curriculum Design*, Croom Helm, 1975

A valuable collection of papers collected as a reader for an OU course on curriculum design and development. The papers have been carefully selected and examine the nature of knowledge, psychological perspectives on the curriculum and approaches to curriculum planning and evaluation. The main arguments of each paper are summarised and an introductory overview provided. See also HARRIS (16).

16 HARRIS, A. et al. (Eds.), *Curriculum Innovation*, Croom Helm, 1975

Comments as per GOLBY (15), with the papers here being organized in terms of 'styles of curriculum development', 'curriculum development at national level', 'curriculum development at local level', 'innovation and the teacher' and 'strategies of innovation'.

17 HOOPER, R. (Ed.), *The Curriculum: Context, Design and Development*, Oliver and Boyd, Edinburgh, 1971

An interesting series of papers of uneven quality and relevance originally collected for the first OU course on the curriculum. A comparison of this collection with those of HARRIS and GOLBY (15 and 16) illustrates changing emphases within curriculum studies and the development of a distinctive English (as opposed to American) tradition.

18 REEDY, S. and WOODHEAD, M. (Eds.), *Family, Work and Education*, Hodder and Stoughton/Open University Press, 1980

A collection of readings concerned with the processes of socialization and learning throughout life. Most of the readings are introductions to, or summaries of research on, topics concerned with childhood, work, ageing, and the future of society. A valuable reminder of the severe limitations of formal curricula in influencing the processes of child and adult socialization.

19 RICHARDS, C. (Ed.), *New Contexts — For Teaching, Learning and Curriculum Studies*, Association for the Study of the Curriculum, Horwich, 1977

A series of conference papers contributed by teachers, lecturers and advisers. Management, innovation, educational policy-making, curriculum research and evaluation are some of the issues discussed. An eclectic, usually readable collection.

20 RICHARDS, C. (Ed.), *Power and the Curriculum*, Nafferton Books, Driffield, 1978

Papers from the Inaugural Conference of the Association for the Study of the Curriculum. Issues examined include curricula as means of social control, educational contraction, difficulties of curriculum reform, testing and accountability and common core curricula. Particularly valuable papers by William Taylor criticizing the 'new' sociology of education, Martin Lightfoot on educational contraction and David Hargreaves on power and the hidden curriculum.

21 RICHARDS, C. (Ed.), *New Directions in Primary Education*, The Falmer Press, Lewes 1982

A collection of papers examining or embodying issues (largely curricular ones) likely to affect primary education in the next decade. Issues discussed include curriculum range, structure, consistency, continuity, evaluation, matching and accountability.

22 RUBIN, L. (Ed.), *Curriculum Handbook*, Allyn and Bacon, Boston, 1977

A two-volume collection of articles (all of them from American sources) dealing with a gamut of educational issues such as accountability, behavioural objectives, open education and the various subjects of the elementary and high school curriculum. Of some relevance but needs to be read in a highly selective fashion. The main points of each paper are neatly summarized and implications (for American theory and practice) drawn out.

23 STENHOUSE, L. (Ed.), *Curriculum Research and Development in Action*, Heinemann, 1980

A collection of case-studies of 15 major curriculum development projects, each of which is appraised by an outsider, whose appraisal in turn is discussed by a representative of the project. An interesting collection but preoccupied with the challenges and problems of the national project era rather than with curriculum research and development in the eighties. Contains a fascinating set of reflections on the 'curriculum movement' by Stenhouse; he suggests that 'like all human endeavours it has to be costed as an aspiration partly realised.... It has stored a lot of capital which will be invested in in-service education in the next decade'. The book contains a very extensive bibliography.

24 TAYLOR, P. (Ed.), *New Directions in Curriculum Studies*, The Falmer Press, Lewes, 1979

Not for the beginner. Contains ten articles (some of them very significant) from the *Journal of Curriculum Studies*, with all too brief editorial introductions to the book as a whole and to each of the three sections: 'The search for new paradigms', 'The ideological dimension' and 'New directions in curriculum research'.

25 TAYLOR, P. and WALTON, J. (Eds.), *The Curriculum: Research, Innovation and Change*, Ward Lock, 1973

A valuable collection of papers from the first Standing Conference on Curriculum Studies and organized under 'practical curriculum development', 'curriculum courses in colleges and universities', 'curriculum research', 'the schools and their curriculum', and 'managing innovation and change'. Papers generally of a good standard with those by Hirst (on the logic of curriculum development) and Musgrove (on curricula for a world of change) being particularly challenging.

26 TAYLOR, P. and TYE. K. (Eds.), *Curriculum, School and Society*, NFER, Windsor, 1975

A 'high-level' introduction for advanced course students. Provides apt but rather terse commentaries on a selection of 16 articles (from *Journal of Curriculum Studies* and *School Review*) dealing with the curriculum as intention and the curriculum in transaction. Useful but highly selective annotated references given.

Other Sources

27 DALE, S., *Using the Literature*, E. 203, *Curriculum Design and Development*, Open University Press, Milton Keynes, 1976

Designed to help OU students acquire the library skills necessary to locate information. Deals clearly and concisely with the use of different libraries, with literature search procedure, with the various bibliographic tools available (e.g. bibliographies, abstracting services, journals) and with organizations associated with the curriculum. A very useful compendium of information and a complement to this annotated bibliography.

28 HARTNETT, A. (Ed.), *The Social Sciences in Educational Studies*, Heinemann, 1982

A source book which provides bibliographic guides to twenty-one areas of educational studies. Some of the guides are little more than lists of publications arranged under headings; others are interesting essays reviewing major trends, documenting published material, and discussing areas for future research. Of particular interest to users of this bibliography are 'Towards a sociology of educational belief' (Hartnett and Naish) 'Ideology and the curriculum' (Apple and Taxel), 'The use of case-studies in applied research and evaluation' (Walker) and 'Towards a sociology of curricular innovation' (Derricott).

29 MORRIS, K., *Curriculum Evaluation: Using the Literature, Curriculum in Action: An Approach to Evaluation*, (P. 234) Open University Press, Milton Keynes, 1981

Similar in approach and value to Dale's guide (27), but more up-to-date and focusing to a greater extent on assessment, evaluation and testing.

30 SCHUBERT, W., *Curriculum Books: The First Eighty Years*, University Press of America, Lanham, 1980

Provides a very comprehensive list of curriculum books published this century, mainly in the United States but also in Britain. Reflects on trends and developments within the literature. The list of books published in the seventies and associated comments are useful for students wishing to extend their reading beyond the material in this bibliography.

31 TYLER, L., *A Selected Guide to Curriculum Literature: An Annotated Bibliography*, National Education Association, Washington DC, 1970

Provides a useful guide to American work in curriculum published in the 50s and 60s. For each article referenced, there is an analysis of its structure, an interpretation and a critique of its contents. No references to British work.

2 The Socio-Cultural Context

Sociology of The Curriculum

32 APPLE, M., 'Commonsense categories and curriculum thought' in *Schooling and Capitalism*, Dale R. *et al.* (Eds), Routledge and Kegan Paul, 1976, 174–184.

Criticizes conventional ways of thinking about pupils and the curriculum, especially the labels applied to children. Argues that the 'scientific' nature of language masks its essentially controlling, dehumanizing functions. Conventional ways of looking at the curriculum are viewed not as politically neutral but as conservative.

33 APPLE, M., *Ideology and Curriculum*, Routledge and Kegan Paul, 1979

A neo-Marxist critique, based largely on revisions of previously published material. Examines unclearly but sometimes insightfully the ideological role of the hidden curriculum, school knowledge and teachers' perspectives in reproducing the social, cultural and economic patterns of capitalist society. Essentially a pessimistic analysis.

34 APPLE, M., 'Social structure, ideology and curriculum', in LAWN, M. and BARTON, L. (Eds.) (see 337) pp. 131–159

A comparatively clear, well-written account of the development of Apple's ideas up to the late seventies. See also (33) and (35).

35 APPLE, M., *Education and Power*, Routledge and Kegan Paul, Boston, 1982

Yet another publication which documents Apple's painful strivings after an adequate understanding of the relationship between education and the surrounding social order. Regards previous analyses as too 'economist and functionalist' with their assumption that schools *only* act to reproduce capitalist social relations. Apple examines some of the contradictions, mediations and resistances which occur in schools and work places and which inhibit the straightforward cultural and social reproduction of dominant class interests. Suggests possibilities for political and educational action in schools to help promote 'progressive structural change' in capitalist societies.

36 ATKIN, J., *The Government in the Classroom*, University of London Institute of Education, 1980

Transcript of a lecture which traces the rapidly growing involvement of government in all levels of education in USA since the war; makes some reference to recent parallel developments in UK. Argues that 'There is little reason to think that government is not in the classroom to stay.' Concludes pessimistically 'if hard times continue (and no one I know is predicting otherwise), my guess is that the quality of public education will continue to slide perceptibly while the government strains to have an ever-greater role in stemming the decline.'

37 BERNBAUM, G. (Ed.), *Schooling in Decline*, Macmillan 1979

A critical examination of the changing position of education (and the changing salience of educational ideologies) in British society in the 70s. A thought-provoking, well-written collection with particularly valuable papers by Bernbaum (editorial introduction), Fowler ('The Politics of Education') and Barrow ('Back to Basics').

38 BERNSTEIN, B., *Towards a Theory of Educational Transmissions, Class Codes and Control*, volume 3, Routledge and Kegan Paul, 1977, (second edition)

A collection of published papers, three of which are specifically concerned with school curricula. There is a long, valuable but very involved introductory chapter putting the papers into perspective. Particularly important are 'On the classification and framing of educational knowledge' which analyzes the organization of educational knowledge and its consequences and 'Class and pedagogies: visible and invisible' which provides a critical examination of the curriculum and pedagogy of the infant school. These papers illustrate Bernstein at his most perceptive and his most inscrutable! See PRING (65).

39 BOURDIEU, P., 'Systems of education and systems of thought', in YOUNG, M.F.D. (Ed.) (74).

An influential, difficult, closely argued paper which establishes a relationship between national intellectual styles and systems of schooling. Schools are seen as a means of transmitting cultural patterns, ways of perceiving, appreciating and thinking. In each thinking individual schooling leaves 'an unthought deposit which underlies all his thoughts'.

40 BOYD-BARRETT, O., *The Curriculum: A Question of Control*, E222, *The Control of Education in Britain*, unit 9, Open University Press, Milton Keynes, 1979

Considers the question 'Who has decided what is taught?' Outlines the range, nature and direction of influences on the curriculum and discusses variations in curriculum control amongst sectors of the educational system.

41 BYRNE HILL, G., 'Some political influences on the curriculum', in KELLY, A. (Ed.), *Curriculum Context*, Harper and Row, 1980 (53)

A valuable article which describes the politics of the curriculum as 'the activity through which state institutions monitor and articulate conflicting views about what children should learn in schools.' Discusses three ways in which the state acts towards education: (i) provision of a recognized minimum of education; (ii) settling and preventing conflicts between interest groups in contested areas of the curriculum; (iii) delegating responsibility through public bodies.

42 CENTRE FOR CONTEMPORARY CULTURAL STUDIES, *Unpopular Education*, Hutchinson, 1981

An interesting and (very largely) readable Marxist analysis of schooling since 1944, especially the 'making' and 'breaking' of social democracy and its educational implications. Part three provides a particularly useful analysis of developments in the 70s.

43 DALE, R., *The Politics of Curriculum Reform*, E. 202, *School and Society*, unit 17, Open University Press, Milton Keynes, 1977

Provides a sociological critique of the curriculum reform movement in England, especially the consequences of the assumptions held by curriculum reformers and the language with which they work. See YOUNG (74) and APPLE (32). Also includes a brief appraisal of the functioning of the Schools Council. More readable than most of the work in the 'new' sociology of education.

44 DALE, R., 'Control, accountability and William Tyndale' in DALE, R. et al. (Eds.), *Politics, Patriarchy and Practice*, The Falmer Press, Open University Press, Lewes, 1981, pp. 305–318

Discusses the impact of the William Tyndale affair on the management of education, teachers' classroom autonomy, and the influence of the teaching profession. Argues that 'While the Tyndale affair did not bring about changes in control, or make accountability necessary, it did have a significant impact on how easily these changes could be made'.

45 DAVIES I., 'Education and social science' in SEAMAN, P., *The Changing Organisation of School Knowledge*, E. 282, *School and Society*, unit 11, Open University Press, Bletchley, 1972

Early paper advocating sociological examination of the school curriculum. Outlines four prominent educational ideologies — 'conservative', 'romantic' 'revisionist and 'democratic socialist'. Clear, concise and incisive.

46 DAVIES, W.B., 'It depends on what you mean by aims', *London Ednl. R.*, 2:3, Autumn 1973, pp. 21–28

A first-rate, memorable, sociological perspective on aims and objectives in education. Starts from the fact that the 'world of education is imprecise, power suffused and value laden' and argues that approaches to the curriculum via aims and objectives are sociologically naive.

47 EGGLESTON, S.J., *The Sociology of the School Curriculum*, Routledge and Kegan Paul, 1977

After discussing a range of sociological approaches the author employs ideological perspectives to analyze the school curriculum. He distinguishes two dominant perspectives (the 'received' and the 'reflexive') and none too clearly advances a 'restructuring' perspective to accommodate them both. Topics discussed include the teacher's role, the sociology of curriculum development and the politics of curriculum knowledge.

48 FOWLER, G., 'The changing nature of educational politics in the 1970s' in BROADFOOT, P. *et al.* (Eds.), *Politics and Educational Change*, Croom Helm, 1984, pp. 13–28

A fascinating analysis by an ex-Minister of State for Education documenting the change from 'disjointed incrementalism' to 'disjointed decrementalism' in educational policy-making and discussing changes in the balance of power both within the 'educational sub-government' and between it and other facets of government.

49 GIROUX, H., *Ideology, Culture and the Process of Schooling*, The Falmer Press, Lewes, 1981

Examines the ideological and political character of the theorizing underlying educational research in the United States. Attempts to develop the foundations of a radical pedagogy which connects 'theory with the need for social action in the interest of individual freedom and social reconstruction'.

50 GRACE, G., *Teachers, Ideology and Control*, Routledge and Kegan Paul, 1978

Focusing on teachers of the urban working class, it provides an examination of their historical origins and formation, and a convincing examination of their contemporary position at the centre of continuing ideological conflict. It draws on Victorian and modern ideological formulations and very interestingly draws out contemporary teachers' implicit theories and the ideologies to which they are linked. Based in part on an analysis of interview data from 105 comprehensive school teachers. The book is a well-rounded whole, a model form which research students could emulate.

51 HUEBNER, D., 'Poetry and power: the politics of curricular development' in PINAR (Ed.) (341) pp. 271–280

The political nature of American schooling exposed in a powerful way. Attacks the propaganda of individualism as 'liberal cant that hides the basic conservatism of school people and permits those who control our public world to continue to control it'. An excellent example of polemical committed theorizing equally applicable to the English context?

52 KAUFMAN, B., 'Piaget, Marx and the political ideology of schooling, *Journal of Curriculum Studies*, 10:1 1978, pp. 19–44

Discusses the relationship between Piaget's developm... ..i psychology and socialist ideology. Argues that there are fundam e il incompatibilities between education based on Piaget' theories and the present structure of Western capitalist society.

53 KELLY, A. (Ed.), *Curriculum Context*, Harper and Row, 1980

A collection of essays which identifies a number of contextual factors constraining curriculum planning. Contributions are of uneven quality and relevance and lack an overall sense of coherence. A particularly interesting paper by Byrne Hill on political influences on the curriculum (41).

54 KIRST, M. and WALKER, D., 'An analysis of curriculum policy-making', *Review of Educational Research*, 41:5, Dec. 1971, pp. 479–510

Curriculum policy-making in the U.S.A. seen as a political activity involving conflict and accommodation among competing groups. Discusses influences and constraints on policy-making and predicts more systematic policy-making.

55 KOGAN, M., *Educational Policy-Making: A study of interest groups and Parliament*, Allen and Unwin, 1975

Provides a history of educational policy-making 1960–74 and classifies the objectives and policies pursued. Considers the part played by LEAS, teachers' associations, parental groups, the media, the Schools Council, and Parliament. Contains a number of case-studies.

56 KOGAN, M., *The Politics of Educational Change*, Fontana, 1978

An excellent, concise overview of the politics of educational change in the 60s and 70s. Discusses current conflicts (e.g. curriculum and standards) and examines the role of local politics, interest groups and central authorities in educational (and curricular) policy-making. An interesting final chapter on future prospects. See also MACLURE (63) and BECHER and MACLURE (175).

57 KOGAN, M. 'Policies for the school curriculum in their political context', *Cambridge Journal of Education*, 11:3, 1980, pp. 122–133

Puts 'A framework for the curriculum' (398) in its political context. Contends that teachers are inevitably in a political game since they have to resolve conflicts between the views of different interest groups about education. 'Good professionals whose expertise includes making sense of multiple values in their client groups cannot avoid politics. They had better master them.'

58 LAWTON, D., *Education and Social Justice*, Sage, 1978

Argues that education should promote social justice through giving all pupils access to worthwhile knowledge. Provides a critique of five educational theories and of the Labour Party's educational record. Presents notes 'towards a theory of democratic educational planning' involving centrally the notion of a core curriculum. Clearly written, but perhaps rather oversimplistic in its critique of educational theories.

59 LAWTON, D., *The Politics of the School Curriculum*, Routledge and Kegan Paul, 1980

The book attempts to trace the change from a 'partnership' model of curriculum control said to characterize education in the 1960s to a complex system of accountability in the 1980s. The book is polemical, makes interesting reading, but contains a large number of unsubstantiated claims.

60 LORTIE, D., *Schoolteacher*, University of Chicago Press, Chicago, 1975

Already a classic sociological study of the American elementary schoolteacher and her 'life-world'. Discusses recruitment to teaching, its rewards, its uncertainties and its purposes. Speculates on future changes and suggests three possible scenarios. A most perceptive study of great value to English teachers and especially to would-be advocates of change.

61 MACDONALD, J. and ZARET, E. (Eds.), *Schools in Search of Meaning*, ASCD, Washington, 1975

A radical critique of American schooling from a Marxist perspective. Especially concerned with posing the question 'In whose interest?' in relation to educational practice. Papers include 'The quality of everyday life in school' (MacDonald) and 'On contradictions in schools' (Mann).

62 MACDONALD, M., *The Curriculum and Cultural Reproduction* I and II, E. 202, *School and Society*, units 18-19, Open University Press, Milton Keynes, 1977

Examines the ways in which the school through its cultural patterns (particularly the ways it selects, organizes and transmits knowledge) allows for the reinforcement and repetition of the social/economic structure. Examines the work of Bernstein, Bourdieu, Marx, Gramsci and Marcuse. Difficult going.

63 MACLURE, S., 'The endless agenda: matters arising', *Oxford Review of Education*, 5:2, 1979, pp. 111-127

An insightful, retrospective examination of the 60s and 70s in terms of (i) numbers and resources, (ii) rise and fall of political expectations, (iii) pedagogic debate, (iv) manpower planning, (v) financing and policy decisions. Concludes: 'there is a need for a fundamental reappraisal of the legal and administrative arrangements for public education, but this is only likely to be fruitful if it follows, rather than precedes, a wider constitutional reform'.

64 MUSGROVE, F., 'Curriculum, culture and ideology', *J. Curriculum Studies*, 10:2, 1978, pp. 99-111

A typical 'swash-buckling' attack on the established wisdom of the 'new' sociology of education. Among other things he disputes the notions of a bourgeois cultural hegemony and of cultural discontinuity for children entering school. Superby written and well-referenced.

65 PRING, R., 'Knowledge out of control?' in GOLBY, M. *et al* (15), pp. 128-137

A powerfully argued critique of the thesis that all knowledge is socially constructed and therefore a construct of particular socio-historical conditions. See YOUNG (74).

66 SALTER, B. and TAPPER, T., *Education, Politics and the State: The Theory and Practice of Educational Change*, Grant McIntyre, 1981

Provides a socio-political theory of educational change — 'a theory which shows how the social and economic pressures for change have to be politically negotiated in the context of state institutions which may, or may not, be sensitive to these pressures and which may have their own ideas as to what constitutes desirable change'. Provides perceptive analyses of the DES ('the state apparatus') and of the Schools Council and has interesting chapters on the Great Debate and its aftermath and on conclusions and future prospects. Refreshingly, non-Marxist in approach, though the views of Marx, Gramsci and Althusser are considered.

67 SCRIMSHAW, P., *Who should control the curriculum?*, E. 200, *Contemporary Issues in Education*, unit 9, Open University Press, Milton Keynes, 1981

Identifies groups exercising some influence over the curriculum in England. Discusses some of the complexities underlying the notion of the 'curriculum' itself and the allied notion of 'curriculum control'. Introduces readers to some of the arguments over central control of the curriculum and teacher accountability.

68 SHARP, R. and GREEN, A., *Education and Social Control: A Study in Progressive Primary Education*, Routledge and Kegan Paul, 1975

A critique of both phenomenological approaches to education (see YOUNG 74) and of child-centred education, based on a year's field-work in a 'progressive' infant school. Modern infant education seen as an aspect of 'romantic radical conservatism'. Book has important things to say but these are obscured by convoluted, over-technical language.

69 WHITESIDE, T., *The Sociology of Educational Innovation*, Methuen, 1978

A useful, clearly written, introductory text which examines attempts to change primary and secondary curricula in England and the United States. Argues there has been far less successful innovation than commonly supposed.

70 WHITTY, G., *School Knowledge and Social Control*, E. 202, *School and Society*, Open University Press, Milton Keynes, units 14–15, 1977

A useful, unusually clear exposition of recent sociological approaches to school knowledge. Provides three interesting case-studies of physics, home economics and music. Recognizes that there has been 'considerable ambiguity and contradiction' within these newer approaches. (See also WHITTY and YOUNG 72)

71 WHITTY, G., *Ideology, Politics and Curriculum*, E. 353, *Society, Education and the State*, unit 8, Open University Press, Milton Keynes, 1981

Discusses the Marxist concept of ideology, including recent attempts to refine the way it is used. Examines the ways in which the curriculum produces meanings and forms of consciousness. Argues that more attention needs to be paid to the political processes through which definitions of curricular knowledge are established and resisted.

72 WHITTY, G. and YOUNG M.F.D., (Eds.), *Explorations in the Politics of School Knowledge*, Nafferton Books, Driffield, 1976

An interesting collection of papers by English sociologists and radical teachers discussing the political character of schooling and the possibilities for its transformation. There are sections on the politics of school subjects (English, music, social studies and science), on the politics of the hidden curriculum, on developing alternatives and on examining the limits to educational change.

73 WILLIAMS, R., *The Long Revolution*, Penguin, Harmondsworth, 1965

Part 2 Chapter One gives an account of the development of English education with particular reference to the effects of social and economic changes. Argues that the present school curriculum was essentially created in the nineteenth century, based on eighteenth century models with elements of a medieval curriculum at its core. Presents a programme of general education for all in order to foster participatory democracy and a common culture of high quality. See also LAWTON (59).

74 YOUNG, M.F.D. (Ed.), *Knowledge and Control*, Collier-Macmillan, 1971

Argues that sociologists should question the fundamental assumptions of current curriculum practice and examine underlying power structures. All knowledge (including the curriculum) is seen as socially constructed. Influential papers by BERNSTEIN (see 38 and 65), Keddie, and Young; a fascinating one by Horton; and difficult ones by Esland and Bourdieu (see 39). The 'sacred book' of the 'New Criticism' described by one critic as 'mind-blowing' in parts! For criticisms see 20 and 65

75 YOUNG, M.F.D., 'The politics of educational knowledge', *Economy and Society*, 1:2, 1972, 194–215

A critique of the Schools Council as an agency of the cultural and social *status quo* denying most working-class pupils access to high-status knowledge. Some sharp, trenchant criticisms blunted by the language in which they are expressed.

Culture and The Curriculum

76 BANTOCK, G., 'Quality and equality in curricular provision' in *Culture, Ideology and Knowledge*, units 3–4, E. 203, *Curriculum Design and Development*, Open University Press, Milton Keynes, 1976

Provides a well-written incisively argued critique of progressivism and developments in the sociology of knowledge. Education is seen as the transmission of culture and as 'by its very nature socially divisive', whilst the curriculum is viewed as differentiated into an academic curriculum for the able and a non-academic curriculum for the majority.

77 BANTOCK, G., *Dilemmas of the Curriculum*, Martin Robertson, Oxford, 1980

An updated restatement and defence of Bantock's views on the elite curriculum and his suggested alternative for those unable to profit from it. Contains an interesting account of the evolution of the curriculum.

78 BANTOCK, G., *The Parochialism of the Present: Contemporary Issues in Education*, Routledge and Kegan Paul, 1981

Contains revised versions of previously published papers (all worth re-reading). Papers include those on discovery methods, equality and education, and 'The parochialism of the present- some reflections on the history of educational theory'.

79 BENJAMIN, H., 'The sabre-tooth curriculum' in HOOPER, R. (Ed.), (17).

A justifiably well-known American curriculum 'fable' dealing amusingly and insightfully with the problems of curriculum change and inertia in a stone-age society. Its message is as pertinent now as when it was first published over forty years ago.

80 CHANAN, G., 'The need for curricular diversity' in SIMON, B. and TAYLOR, W. (Eds.), *Education in the Eighties: The Central Issues*, Batsford Educational, 1981

Argues against standardization and for the provision of experimental variations within the curriculum, not just in peripheral options but also in central areas. Argues the need to build in many areas of contemporary life and to bring students' emotional life to the centre of the educational enterprise.

81 CHANAN, G. and GILCHRIST, L., *What School Is For*, Methuen, 1974

Short, thought-provoking book examining the cultures of the school, of pupils and of the middle class and arguing that schools need to be reconstituted as workshops for the creation of a new culture of 'universal humanitarianism'. But see 76 and 77.

82 GOLBY, M. (Ed.), *The Core Curriculum*, Perspectives 2, School of Education, University of Exeter, 1980

A valuable set of papers analyzing, from a variety of viewpoints, aspects of the 'core curriculum' debate. Issued to sharpen discussion following the publication of the DES document *A Framework for the School Curriculum* (398). Papers range from the journalistic to the academic, but the book as a whole is well worth reading.

83 REYNOLDS, J. and SKILBECK, M., *Culture and the Classroom*, Open Books, 1976

Explores the relationships between culture and curriculum with particular emphasis on the cultural significance of curriculum decisions. Though uneven in quality, it has useful chapters on values, beliefs and culture, on ideology and culture and on schools and the curriculum design process. In the final chapter is an interesting proposal for a common core cultural curriculum.

84 SKILBECK, M., 'The school and cultural development', in GOLBY (15) pp. 27-35

Outlines four possible strategies for schools to adopt in the light of social change. Advocates a reconstructionist ideology of education and a curriculum based on the study and appraisal of contemporary culture. See REYNOLDS and SKILBECK (83).

85 SKILBECK, M., *Ideologies and Values*, E. 203, *Curriculum Design and Development*, Open University Press, Milton Keynes, 1976

A useful clearly written introduction to the concepts of culture, ideology and value. It discusses classical humanism (see BANTOCK 77), progressivism and reconstructionism as examples of educational ideologies and examines the question of what values should be embodied in the school curriculum.

86 STENHOUSE, L., *Culture and Education*, Nelson, 1967

Argues that 'the central purpose of education' is 'to transmit culture through the symbols which make it accessible to criticism and creative thinking'. Contains many of Stenhouse's ideas, later elaborated in more tangible form through his participation in the curriculum development movement.

87 WARNOCK, M., *Schools of Thought*, Faber, 1977

Takes a number of important central issues (the distribution of education, equality as a curriculum aim, curriculum structure) and examines how far each is purely educational and how far wider issues of values are involved.

Argues that decisions about the curriculum necessitate a commitment to values. Educational decisions are seen to be both political and moral.

88 WHITE, J., *Towards a Compulsory Curriculum*, Routledge and Kegan Paul, 1973

A closely reasoned, thought-provoking argument for a compulsory curriculum. Children to be compelled to engage in certain activities (where understanding presupposes engagement) and to understand something of different ways of life. On this basis they can rationally choose a life-pattern to pursue. Not always easy reading but an important book.

89 WHITE, J., *The Aims of Education Restated*, Routledge and Kegan Paul, 1982

A re-examination of the aims of education drawing on the views of other writers but going beyond these to develop and justify the argument that the central aim of education is to develop morally virtuous and autonomous persons. Has a final chapter in which he sketches out how that aim might be realized in practice.

3 Curriculum History

(Compiled by David Hamilton, Department of Education, University of Glasgow)

90 BALL, S.J., 'Competition and conflict in the teaching of English: a socio-historical analysis,' *Journal of Curriculum Studies*, 1982, 14:1, pp. 1–28

Describes the networks of communication and scholarship that have created the various paradigms for teaching English that exist today.

91 DAVIE, G.E., *The Democratic Intellect: Scotland and her Universities in the Nineteenth Century*, Edinburgh University Press, 1961

A pioneering study of curricular reform in higher education written as an analysis of the anglicisation of the Scottish educational system. Critics argue that Davie has overplayed the importance of external forces and underplayed the internal dynamics of Scotland at that time.

92 DURKHEIM, E., *The Evolution of Educational Thought: Lectures on the Formation and Development of Secondary Education in France*, Routledge & Kegan Paul, 1977

Although some of the historical data is in need of revision, Durkheim's lectures — delivered in 1904–5 — still provide valuable insight into the interpretation and analysis of curriculum change in particular and educational and social change in general.

93 GOODSON, I., *School Subjects and Curriculum Change*, Croom Helm, 1982

Provides a valuable socio-historical analysis of school subjects: both of their definition and evolution and of their promotion and selection within the secondary school curriculum since the late nineteenth century. Includes case studies of geography, biology, rural studies and environmental studies.

94 GORDON, P. & LAWTON, D., *Curriculum Change in the Nineteenth and Twentieth Centuries*, Hodder & Staughton, 1978

Tends to focus on the administrative origins of curriculum change (i.e. through legislative channels) but nevertheless gives a worthwhile view of the 'prehistory' of contemporary curricula.

95 HAMILTON, D. & GIBBONS, M., 'Notes on the origins of the educational terms "class" and "curriculum",'. Paper presented at the 1980 Meeting of the American Educational Research Association, Boston (*ERIC* No. *ED 183 453*)

A speculative paper which, in the absence of contrary data suggests that the earliest known appearances of curriculum (at Leiden and Glasgow Universities) can be linked to the educational ideologies of Calvinism. The modern meaning comes from the latin word for a race-track via the intermediate form *curriculum vitae* (course of life). A central assumption of the earliest uses was that a curriculum retained both a sequential and an overarching structure.

96 KLIEBARD, H.M., 'The drive for curriculum change in the United States, 1890–1958,' *Journal of Curriculum Studies*, 1979, 11.3, pp. 191–202, 11.4, pp. 273–286.

A two part review: 'The ideological roots of curriculum as a field of specialization' and 'From local reform to a national preoccupation'. A schematic but valuable review of the context of curriculum theory and practice in the USA.

97 LAYTON, D., *Science for the People: the Origins of the School Science Curriculum in England*, Allen & Unwin, 1973

A pioneering work, like DAVIE's *The Democratic Intellect* (see 91) which examines the intellectual debates and context of late nineteenth century schooling. Can also be read as an essay on the secularization of the school curriculum.

98 MARSDEN, W.E. (Ed.), *Post-war Curriculum Development: an Historical Appraisal*, History of Education Society, Leicester, 1979

Proceedings of the Society's 1978 conference with papers on middle schools, biology, higher education, the United States and West Germany. Concludes with an essay on historical approaches to curriculum study and an extensive bibliographic essay on recent work.

99 SEGUEL, M.L., *The Curriculum Field: Its Formative Years*, Teachers College Press, New York, 1966

Examines the period 1895–1937 through the work of a series of key innovators. Gives a broad overview of some of the context and choices that have exercised educationists during the period of the rise of the United States to a position of intellectual dominance in the field of curriculum studies.

100 WATSON, F., *The Beginnings of the Teaching of Modern Subjects in England*, Scolar Press, 1971 (originally published in 1909)

Records details of the changeover from medieval (i.e. Latin-based) to modern (vernacular-based) curricula in the 15–17th centuries. At the same time it stands as a valuable, base-line study of the emergence of the text-book (ratter than a source-text) as a central artefact of schooling.

4 Curriculum Agents and Agencies

National

101 BELL, R. and PRESCOTT, W. (Eds.), *The Schools Council: A Second Look*, Ward Lock, 1975

A valuable collection of papers reviewing the Schools Council's first ten years of operation. Papers mostly reprinted elsewhere but a few original ones including Pring on integration, Mothersole on publishing and MacLure on examinations. Dated in view of developments since 1975.

102 BLACKIE, J., *Inspecting and the Inspectorate*, Routledge and Kegan Paul, 1970

One of the very few accounts of the work of the inspectorate — seen from an insider's perspective. Rather uncritical as a result. An extra chapter now needs to be written in view of the recent stronger, more public stance taken by the inspectorate on curriculum matters (see the paper by BROWNE in LELLO (293)).

103 CERI, *Case-Studies of Educational Innovation: 1. At the Central Level*, OECD, Paris, 1973

Contains case-studies of seven national agencies set up in Western Europe and America to promote educational change. Nisbet's long contribution on the Schools Council is a valuable analysis, though, by now, many of his most apposite comments have been overtaken by events.

104 KOGAN, M. and PACKWOOD, T., *Advisory Councils and Committees in Education*, Routledge and Kegan Paul, 1974

Examines the nature and impact of advisory bodies and committees on decision-making in education. Discusses the main themes underlying the work of major councils (1920–72), examines four reports in detail (including the Crowther and Plowden Reports) and speculates on the future of advisory systems. A much needed contribution in a neglected area.

105 MACDONALD, G., 'The politics of educational publishing' in WHITTY, G. and YOUNG, M.F.D. (Eds). (72), pp. 223–235

One of the few articles available on the role of publishers in education (See also MOTHERSOLE 101). Argues that publications represent diffuse but powerful mechanisms of social control. Describes attempts to publish material outside the prevailing consensus of publishers and the educational establishment.

106 PRESCOTT, W, *Innovation at the National Level*, E. 203, *Curriculum Design and Development*, unit 24, Open University Press, Milton Keynes, 1976

Provides a good summary of the Schools Council — its origins, its work on examinations, the views of its supporters and its critics, and its possible alternative futures. A sketchier section also provided on the work of examination boards. See also RICHARDS (107) NISBET (in 103) and WYATT (111).

107 RICHARDS, C., 'The Schools Council: A Critical Examination', *Universities Q.*, 28:3, pp. 323–336, Summer 1974

Argues that the Schools Council is a prisoner of its own assumptions and outmoded development strategies and that it reflects, rather than challenges, conventional wisdom. Suggests the regionalization of curriculum development and the establishment of a national 'think-tank' appraising fundamentals in a radical way. See also NISBET (in 103) and BELL and PRESCOTT (101).

108 TRENAMAN, N., *Review of the Schools Council*, Department of Education and Science, 1981

Appraises the work of the Schools Council in the light of evidence collected personally and submitted by other interested parties. Though critical in many respects, it recommends that 'the Schools Council should continue and with its present functions'.

109 WARING, M., *Social Pressures and Curriculum Innovation*, Methuen, 1979

A study of the Nuffield Foundation Science Teaching Project, with a particular focus on the development of the O-level chemistry curriculum. Draws on much previously unpublished material to document the setting up of the Project, its mode of operation and its outcomes. Rather dense reading in parts, but does throw some light on an important aspect of the history of curriculum studies in the United Kingdom.

110 WHITE, J. (Ed.), *No Minister*, Bedford Way Papers, 4, University of London Institute of Education, 1981

A motley collection of critical papers — perhaps too instant a response to the publication of the DES document *The School Curriculum* (398).

Contains a particularly well argued paper by Aspin 'Utility is not enough: the arts in the school curriculum'.

111 WYATT, T., 'The GCE examining boards and curriculum development' in HARRIS et al, (16), pp. 104–114

An interesting 'apologetic' account which indicates the ways in which exam boards have responded to curriculum changes and which considers constraints limiting boards' initiative.

Local

112 ADAMS, E. (Ed.), *Inservice Education and Teachers' Centres*, Oxford, Pergamon, 1975

A collection of papers outlining the past, present and future role of advisers, teachers' centres and colleges in the inservice education of teachers. Contains a particularly interesting contribution by Skilbeck where he elaborates his views on school-based curriculum development and its necessary support structures.

113 BELL, R., *Some Outside Forces*, E. 283, *The Curriculum: Context, Design and Development*, unit 15, Open University Press, Bletchley, 1972

A useful examination of the role of local education authorities in curriculum improvement based on a paper by OWEN (see 193) drawing on his experience as an administrator in Devon and on a paper by Humble and Rudduck writing as members of the Humanities Curriculum Project team.

114 BERESFORD, C., 'Teachers' centre processes and inservice opportunities', *Cambridge J. Ed.*, 4:2, 1974, pp. 93–101

An insightful article reappraising the role of teachers' centre wardens. Sees them not as dispensers of hardware nor as salesmen for projects, but as developers of communications networks and facilitators of the further professional development of teachers.

115 BOLAM, R., *Innovation at Local Level*, E. 203, *Curriculum Design and Development*, unit 25, Open University Press, Milton Keynes, 1976

An uneven, incomplete examination of curriculum development at the local level but containing a particularly useful section on advisers. Always clear and readable. See also BOLAM (116).

116 BOLAM, R. et al., *LEA Advisers and the Mechanisms of Innovation*, NFER, Windsor, 1978
Considers: the major tasks of advisers, advisers and innovation, and the problems of liaison, communication and working contacts. Also contains three case studies of advisers attempting to bring about change in schools.

117 CERI, *Case-Studies of Educational Innovation: 2. At the Regional Level*, O.E.C.D., Paris, 1973
Discusses how educational change has been fostered at regional level by reference to five case-studies including two of Leicestershire and Devon. These are somewhat disappointing, lacking the detailed analysis characteristic of Nisbet's work on the Schools Council (103).

118 CERI, *Case-Studies of Educational Innovation: 3. At School Level*, O.E.C.D., Paris, 1973
The third volume of case-studies (see 103 and 117) dealing with change in schools. Five case-studies are presented, all at secondary level, including Bernbaum's account of the situation at Countesthorpe School in its early days.

119 DICKINSON, N., 'The headteacher as innovator: a study of an English school district' in REID, W. and WALKER, D. (Eds). (194) pp. 136–178
A series of short case-studies plus analyses of the role of headteachers in introducing changes in Hull during a period of re-organization to a three-tier system. It shows how heads handle suggestions for change and manage the adaptive process which follows a decision for adoption. Rather than promoting radical change, heads allow for modifications of existing structures within well-defined and familiar parameters.

120 GILCHRIST, G., 'Local support for innovation', *British Journal of Teacher Education*, 4:1, 1978 pp. 55–68
Suggests a typology of local support systems based on three types of agency role: 'authoritative', 'informative' and 'supportive'. Briefly considers the infrastructure created by the Geography for the Young School Leaver project. Argues that local support systems need to 'be better understood, stronger and more adequately financed'.

121 GLATTER, R. (Ed.), *Control of the Curriculum-Issues and Trends in Britain and Europe, Studies in Education 2*, NFER, Windsor, 1977
A series of conference papers discussing the part played by various agencies in decision-making about the curriculum in a sample of

European countries — England, Scotland, France, Germany and Scandinavia. Also contains a review of issues raised about curriculum control by Fowler.

122 REDKNAP, C., *Focus On Teachers' Centres*, NFER, Windsor, 1977

Usefully draws together a great deal of material on teachers' centres not readily accessible before. See also ADAMS (112) and BERESFORD (114).

5 Curriculum Design

General

123 BARROW, R., *Common Sense and the Curriculum*, Allen and Unwin, 1976

Argues for a common curriculum justified in terms of utilitarianism. Provides critical comments on the curriculum theories of Hirst, Bantock, Neil, Goodman and White. Produces his own positive theory and details a practical programme to implement it.

124 BROUDY, H. et al., *Democracy and Excellence in American Secondary Education*, Rand McNally, Chicago, 1964

A very sound, coherently argued position in relation to curriculum design. The principles and arguments are of wide applicability, not merely to secondary education. The early chapters are particularly useful.

125 BRUNER, J., *The Process of Education*, Harvard University Press, Cambridge, 1960

A clear, beautifully written account which summarizes Bruner's early views on the curriculum (especially his notions of 'structure' and 'the spiral curriculum'). It has proved very influential and, unlike many American texts, is short and compact.

126 DEARDEN, R., 'Balance and coherence: some curricular principles in recent reports', *Cambridge Journal of Education*, 11:2, 1981, pp. 107–118

An interesting, clearly written paper which considers the merits of 'balance' and 'coherence' as curricular principles. Gets behind the rhetoric of recent reports. Analyzes the two concepts and their presuppositions.

127 EISNER, E. and VALLANCE E. (Eds.), *Conflicting Conceptions of Curriculum*, McCutcheon, Berkeley, 1974

A collection illustrating five different orientations to curriculum, as evidenced in the United States. The authors describe these clearly and succinctly in their introduction and apply them to 'Man: A Course of Study' in their concluding chapter. The papers are of uneven quality and difficulty; the ones by Bereiter and Schwab are particularly interesting.

128 HIRST, P., *Knowledge and the Curriculum*, Routledge and Kegan Paul, 1974

A collection of Hirst's papers raising crucial questions about the nature of knowledge. The book details Hirst's views (and defence) of forms of knowledge and their implications for curriculum planning. Particularly useful papers on philosophy and curriculum planning, on the nature and structure of curriculum objectives and on curriculum integration.

129 INGLIS, F., 'Ideology and the Curriculum: the value assumptions of system builders', *J. Curriculum Studies*, 6:1, May 1974, pp. 3–14

A critique of technical, consensual curriculum planning as exemplified by Merritt, Hirst and Peters, and Bruner. Argues that such thinking avoids discussion of the moral ends of education and of conflicts inherent in the human condition.

130 KING, A. and BROWNELL, J., *The Curriculum and the Disciplines of Knowledge*, Wiley, New York, 1966

Mainly known for its coherent and thoughtful justification of basing the curriculum on making an 'Intellectual Man' rather than a 'Political', 'Religious', 'Social' or 'Economic' man. By defending the curricular *status quo* it helps show the latter's present assumptions more clearly.

131 PARKER, J. and RUBIN., L., *Process as Content*, Rand McNally, Chicago, 1966

A carefully worked out argument for the selection of content in terms of the cognitive processes to be revealed. A useful model provided of three kinds of operations in a process-centred curriculum: intake operations (*e.g.* listening, listing), manipulative operations (*e.g.* comparing, verifying) and applicative operations (*e.g.* solving). Examples given in English, geography, mathematics, physics and social studies.

132 PHENIX, P., *Realms of Meaning*, McGraw Hill, New York, 1964

Phenix develops a philosophy of the curriculum based on the notion that human beings are essentially creatures who have the power to create and express meanings. He analyzes six 'realms of meaning' and draws out the significance of this analysis for curriculum design. For criticism of his views see a paper in HIRST (128).

133 PRATT, D., *Curriculum: Design and Development*, Harcourt, Brace Jovanovich, New York, 1980

A Canadian text for undergraduate and graduate students. Details the curricular decisions involved in planning, starting with the consideration of significant human needs and ending with the implementation of curricula in classrooms. Most chapters usefully begin with a list of the principles and concepts to be covered. A variety of amusing and/or insightful aphorisms lighten the text. A book to be used very selectively, not worked through cover to cover.

134 PRING, R., *Knowledge and Schooling*, Open Books, 1976

Examines several approaches to the place of knowledge in the curriculum: the philosophical arguments for forms of knowledge; the sociology of knowledge (a very useful critique), the claims for an interest-based curriculum; the different senses of curriculum integration; and Pring's own analysis of 'commonsense knowledge'. A well-written and valuable synthesis, though not for the absolute beginner in the field.

135 ROWNTREE, D., *Educational Technology in Curriculum Development* (second edition) Harper and Row, 1982

Presents educational technology as a rational, problem solving approach to education, a way of thinking sceptically and systematically about learning and teaching. Considers (i) objectives, (ii) content, sequence and strategy, (iii) modes and media, (iv) evaluation and improvement, (v) the role of educational technology.

136 SCHOOLS COUNCIL, *The Practical Curriculum*, Working Paper 70, Methuen, 1981

An attempt to distil, for practising teachers, principles for the planning, monitoring and assessment of the school curriculum. Loosely put together and fails to provide a body of defensible curriculum principles. Nevertheless, some useful pragmatic suggestions are hidden away within the text. Written by a committee and it shows!

137 SKILBECK, M., 'Core curriculum — a fresh approach', *Primary Education Review*, 12, 1981, pp. 15-18

A brief but cogent critique of recent moves by the DES to establish a national framework for the curriculum. Argues the need for a framework but one based on cultural mapping (see 83).

138 SOCKETT, H., 'Curriculum planning: taking a means to an end', in PETERS, R. (Ed.), *The Philosophy of Education*, Oxford University Press, Oxford, 1973, pp. 150-160

A difficult paper which criticizes the behavioural objectives model of curriculum planning as based on a very restricted conception of means-ends connections. Five such connections are discussed in place of the one stressed by advocates of curriculum planning by behavioural objectives.

139 SOCKETT, H., *Approaches to Curriculum Planning 1*, E. 203, *Curriculum Design and Development*, unit 16, Open University Press, Milton Keynes, 1976

After hurriedly considering the views of Mill, Oakshott and Dewey on rational activity, he summarizes the main features of so-called 'rational' curriculum planning involving the specification of behavioural objectives and then provides a critique of this.

140 SOCKETT, H., *Approaches to Curriculum Planning 2*, E. 203, *Curriculum Design and Development*, unit 17, Open University Press, Milton Keynes, 1976

Considers amendments to the rational planning model (139) by examining in detail the approach of Science 5–13 to curriculum design. Outlines all too briefly alternative planning models. Fails to draw out many practical principles for teachers attempting to design their own curricula.

141 SOCKETT, H., *Designing the Curriculum*, Open Books, 1976

A very good introduction to the problems and possibilities of curriculum design. Provides a well-argued critique of 'rational' curriculum planning through objectives. Suggests the notion of designing the structure of the curriculum as it is and making piecemeal improvements in the light of this design. Such improvements might be effected by giving attention to objectives or content or procedural principles or teaching methods.

142 STENHOUSE, L., *An Introduction to Curriculum Research and Development*, Heinemann, 1975

Of particular relevance to curriculum design are the chapters on behavioural objectives and curriculum development, on a critique of behavioural objectives and on the 'process' model

143 TYLER, R., *Basic Principles of Curriculum and Instruction*, University of Chicago Press, Chicago, 1949

In what is now a classic text Tyler outlines his 'rational' planning model for curriculum design. Sections deal with ways of formulating, organizing and evaluating the educational objectives that have been chosen for the curriculum.

144 WHITFIELD, R. (Ed.), *Disciplines of the Curriculum*, McGraw Hill, 1971

A collection of papers, from a variety of contributors, on the nature of school subjects, which the editor attempts to synthesize to produce a 'blueprint' for the 9–16 curriculum. Interesting to re-examine this attempt a decade or so on.

Objectives-based designs, critiques and alternatives

145 ATKIN, M., 'Behavioural objectives in curriculum design: a cautionary note', *The Science Teacher*, 35, 1968, pp. 27–30

A short, early and influential critique. Doubts whether the multitude of educational objectives can readily be identified. Argues that objectives may hinder innovation and teacher spontaneity. Stresses that the worthwhileness of goals is independent of their measurability.

146 BLOOM, B. et al., *Taxonomy of Educational Objectives: Handbook 1: Cognitive Domain*, Longmans, 1973

A paperback edition of Bloom's influential book which attempts to classify educational objectives in terms of the behaviour of the learner. His learning hierarchy begins with simple operations and proceeds to complex levels of understanding in the cognitive area. Has come in for considerable criticism from philosophers (see 153 and 160). More a work of reference than a book to be read from cover to cover.

147 BLYTH, W. et al., *Place, Time and Society 8–13: Curriculum Planning in History, Geography and Social Science*, Collins/ESL, Glasgow/Bristol, 1976

An interesting variant on 'hard-line' 'rational' curriculum planning. Details an approach to planning involving the selection of key concepts (e.g. values, communication) and the use of objectives. A clear, readable, non-technical exposition which provides detailed examples of the design process advocated.

148 DAVIES, I., *The Management of Learning*, McGraw-Hill, 1971

Applies management concepts to educational technology in general and to teaching and training in particular. Has four sections: 'Planning', 'Organising', 'Leading' and 'Controlling'. Regards teachers as managers of learning resources, charged with the role of deciding between alternative teaching and learning strategies. Described by one reviewer as 'A book about training, by a trainer, for trainers'. With its concern for task analysis, learning objectives and teaching strategies and tactics, the book is more 'hard-nosed' and behaviouristic than the author's later book (149).

149 DAVIES, I., *Objectives in Curriculum Design*, McGraw-Hill, 1976

Provides a rationale for thinking about, and working with, objectives. The author argues that objectives are not a panacea, but are useful tools, more helpful in some situations than others. Section One discusses the assumptions underlying objectives, arguments for and against using them and a review of research findings. Section Two discusses how objectives can be used and organised. Presents objectives 'with a human face'.

150 EISNER, E., 'Educational objectives: help or hindrance?', *School Review*, 75, 1967, pp. 250–260

A seminal article which challenges the assumption that objectives have to be stated clearly, unambiguously and specifically in terms of pupils' behaviour or performance. Drawing on his experience of curriculum work in the visual arts he produces four major criticisms. In summary he suggests that 'in large measure the construction of curriculums and the judgement of their consequences are artful tasks'.

151 EISNER, E., 'Instructional and expressive educational objectives' in POPHAM, W. (Ed.), *Instructional Objectives*, AERA, Monograph 3, Rand McNally, Chicago, 1969 pp. 1–18

After outlining three dominant metaphors in American education ('industrial', 'behavioural' and 'biological') he distinguishes 'instructional objectives' specifying terminal pupil behaviour and 'expressive objectives' which identify learning situations but do not specify what children are to learn from these.

152 EISNER, E., 'Emerging models for educational evaluation', *School Review*, 80, 1972, pp. 573–90

Another clear, well-written piece outlining Eisner's developing thoughts on evaluation. In addition to 'instructional' and 'expressive objectives' he suggests a third type which describes problematic situations to which there are a variety of solutions meeting specified criteria, but leaves the actual resolution of these situations to pupil initiative. (See 10, 150 and 151.)

153 GRIBBLE, J., 'Pandora's Box: the affective domain of educational objectives', *J. Curriculum Studies* 2:1, May 1970, pp. 11–24

A critique of Bloom and Krathwohl's taxonomies (146 and 155). Raises questions of whether (a) an educational taxonomy can be neutral and (b) the cognitive and affective domains can valuably be separated.

154 HOGBEN, D., 'The behavioural objectives approach: some problems and some dangers', *J. Curriculum Studies*, 4:1, 1972, pp. 42–50

Points out the dangers of too exclusive a concentration on objectives stated in highly specific behavioural terms. Has useful suggestions for teachers and curriculum workers interested in objectives. Very clear and readable.

155 KRATHWOHL, D., BLOOM, B., et al., *Taxonomy of Educational Objectives: Handbook 2: Affective Domain*, Longmans, 1973

See BLOOM (146). Attempts classification of affective objectives in terms of a hierarchy from 'receiving' through 'responding', 'valuing', 'organization' to 'characterization by a value or value-complex'. Has come in for severe philosophical criticism (*e.g.* 153 and 160), but influential nevertheless. Difficult reading.

156 MACDONALD-ROSS, M., 'Behavioural objectives: a critical review' in GOLBY, M. *et al* (15), pp. 355–386

Details a large number of difficulties inherent in the use of behavioural objectives and contends that the claims made for such objectives are weakened or negated by these criticisms. An impressive critique.

157 MAGER, R., *Preparing Instructional Objectives*, Feanon, Palo Alto, 1962

A short concise guide to preparing behavioural objectives. In a way too readable, gives the reader too simplistic a view of what objectives' prespecification involves. Nevertheless states the case in a powerful, but entertaining, way.

158 POPHAM, W., 'Objectives '72', in RUBIN, (Ed.), (22), pp. 605–613

A foremost advocate of planning by instructional objectives, he reviews the objectives controversy in the United States. Accepts there have been abuses of objectives-based planning but still supports the basic approach. Argues that attempts to clarify and assess the more profound goals of education are worth making, and contends that 'most educational goals can be operationalized'.

159 PRATT, D., 'Humanistic goals and behavioural objectives: towards a synthesis' *J. Curriculum Studies*, 8:1, May 1976, pp. 15–26

A valuable attempt at creating a synthesis from humanistic and behavioural approaches to curriculum design. Argues that their thinking is much closer than either group believes, that both have contributions to make to discussion of goals and that equally both have deficiencies.

160 PRING, R., 'Bloom's taxonomy: a philosophical critique (2)', *Cambridge J. Ed.*, 1:2, Easter 1971, pp. 83–91

Criticizes Bloom's taxonomy (146 and 155) for not being based on epistemological analysis. Argues that the taxonomy distorts by separating the cognitive and affective domains, and by differentiating knowledge from intellectual abilities.

161 RATHS, J., 'Teaching without specific objectives', *Educational Leadership*, 28:7, 1971, pp. 714–720

Criticizes teaching for objectives as dull and stultifying but accepts that some such teaching is necessary. As an alternative to selecting activities in the light of pre-specified objectives, he provides twelve criteria 'for identifying activities that seem to have some inherent worth'.

162 REYNOLDS, J. and SKILBECK, M., *Culture and the Classroom*, Open Books, 1976

See chapter five for an outline of a 'situational' model for curriculum planning involving five stages. Such a model can usefully encompass both 'objectives-based' and 'process' approaches to planning. (See also 9)

163 SOCKETT, H., 'Behavioural objectives', *London Ednl. R.*, 2:3, Autumn 1973, pp. 38–45

A brief but difficult philosophical critique of behavioural objectives. Discusses the 'ambiguities and absurdities' of operationalism, the restrictions of methodological behaviourism and the implications of a verification theory of meaning, all of which underlie approaches to curriculum planning using behavioural objectives.

164 STENHOUSE, L., et al., *The Humanities Curriculum Project: An Introduction*, Heinemann, 1970

A handbook for teachers outlining the rationale of the Humanities Curriculum Project and giving principles of procedure for teachers to adopt in handling controversial issues with adolescents. A practical exemplification of Stenhouse's process model (see also 12).

model. Outlines a form or principles model to curriculum planning which begins with the specification of content, not objectives. Views rational curriculum planning not in Tylerian terms (143) but as the exercise of cautious judgment in making decisions to achieve a coordinated curriculum in the presence of so many variables and uncertainties.

Psychology and Curriculum Design

166 AUSUBEL, D. et al., *Educational Psychology: A Cognitive View*, (second edition), Holt, Rinehart and Winston, New York, 1978

Focusses on what Ausubel terms meaningful 'reception' and 'discovery' learning. The cognitive, affective and social factors influencing meaningful verbal learning are examined. Its critique of Bruner's views on discovery learning are particularly interesting (and hard-hitting!).

167 BRUNER, J., *Towards a Theory of Instruction*, Belknap Press, Cambridge, 1966

A collection of papers, all readable and valuable. Paper 3 ('Notes on a theory of instruction') and paper 4 (Man: a course of study) are particularly valuable, the first as an exposition of the principles underlying Bruner's thinking on the curriculum and the second as an embodiment of these principles in a curriculum project. See also BRUNER (125)

168 DONALDSON, M., *Children's Minds*, Fontana, 1978

Argues that largely because of the influence of Piaget's work we have underestimated the rational powers of young children, who can perform complex tasks given a setting and a language that makes sense to them. Too often the activities comprising the school curriculum do not provide such a setting or language.

169 FLOYD, A. (Ed.), *Cognitive Development in the School Years*, Croom Helm/Open University Press, 1979

A collection of articles dealing with research in cognitive development and the relevance of this research to educational practice. Part Four is particularly useful, as it deals with the implications of cognitive development for social studies (Derricott and Blyth), primary science (Harlen), the Nuffield O-level Physics course (Shayer) and the learning of mathematics (Brown).

170 FLOYD, A., *Development in the School Years*, E. 362, *Cognitive Development*, Block 3, Open University Press, Milton Keynes, 1979

Largely concerned with discussing the development of children's performance on a wide range of tasks in the laboratory situation. Then, by reference to science, social studies, maths and pre-school provision, it illustrates (all too briefly) how curricula can be designed to take account of cognitive-development psychology. Needs to be read in conjunction with the papers in the reader edited by FLOYD (169).

171 GAGNÉ, R., *The Conditions of Learning*, (third edition) Holt Rinehart and Winston, New York, 1977

This third edition, very different in orientation from the first two, discusses the nature of, and conditions of learning for, five types of capability: intellectual skills, cognitive strategies, verbal information, motor skills and attitudes. The final two chapters apply principles and concepts to the design and development of programmes of instruction.

172 GAMMAGE, P. and GREENWALD, J., *Human Development and the Curriculum*, E. 203, *Curriculum Design and Development*, unit 6 Open University Press, Milton Keynes, 1976

A straightforward overview of the contribution of psychology to curriculum thinking. Better when dealing with the more direct influences of Skinner, Piaget and Bruner than with the indirect influences of Freud and Erikson. Has a useful historical section on changing perspectives of childhood.

173 HARNISCHFEGER, A. and WILEY, D., 'The teaching-learning process in elementary schools: a synoptic view'. *Curriculum Inquiry*, 6:1, 1976, pp. 5–44

An influential model of the teaching-learning process based on the conviction that 'the quantity of education determines the outcomes of pedagogy in fundamental and powerful ways'. In particular, it argues that 'The total amount of actual learning time on a particular instructional topic is the most important determinant of the pupil's achievement on that topic'.

174 SOULSBY, D., 'Gagné's hierarchical theory of learning: some conceptual difficulties', *J. Curriculum Studies*, 7:2, 1975, pp. 122–132

An interesting, well-argued critique.

6 Curriculum Development

General

175 BECHER, T. and MACLURE, S., *The Politics of Curriculum Change*, Hutchinson, 1978

A well-written, thought-provoking analysis of curriculum development since 1945. It introduces a number of new concepts which help make sense of the complexities of development activities. Has particularly interesting chapters on the 'politics of acceptability' and the 'dynamics of the public curriculum'. (See 56, 63 and 189)

176 BOLAM, R., 'The management of educational change: towards a conceptual framework', in HARRIS, A. *et al.* (16), pp. 273–290

Provides a simple but usable organizing framework for studying educational innovation. It has two major dimensions — one dealing with the major systems of change-agent, innovation and user, and the other dealing with three phases of innovation over time. The framework is briefly and inadequately applied to the Teacher Induction Pilot Schemes Project.

177 BROWN, S. and MCINTYRE, D., 'Factors influencing teachers' responses to curricular innovations' *Research Intelligence*, 4:1, 1978, pp. 19–23

Analyzes teachers' responses to the introduction of Scottish Integrated Science. Suggests some principles to guide would-be innovators but accepts that 'The possibility of uncovering a recipe for a general innovation strategy is remote.'

178 CERI, *Case-Studies of Educational Innovation: 4. Strategies for Innovation in Education*, OECD, Paris, 1973

The summary volume to the CERI case-studies (103, 117 and 118). Provides a theoretical framework which it applies to the studies. Has interesting chapters on the individual and innovation and on barriers and unintended effects.

179 CERI, *Handbook on Curriculum Development*, OECD, Paris, 1975

A compilation of contributions of uneven quality which, taken together, provide a useful international perspective on curriculum development. The 'art' of development, its administrative and social settings, case-studies (very short) of selected projects and valuable reflections on the nature of curriculum studies are included. (See also 190 and 197.)

180 DALIN, P., *Limits to Educational Change*, Macmillan, 1978

An overview of theoretical models and analyses. Makes rather dull reading but parts are useful *e.g.* barriers to change, theories and models of educational change, and change as mutual adaptation and development.

181 HARDING, J., KELLY, P. and NICODEMUS, R., 'The study of curriculum change', *Studies in Science Education*, 3, pp. 1–30, 1976

A useful overview of some of the dissemination and adoption studies conducted in this country and the United States.

182 HARLEN, W., 'A stronger teacher role in curriculum development', *J. Curriculum Studies*, 9:1, 1977, pp. 21–30

The strength of teacher participation in the curriculum development process is discussed in terms of (a) research roles, and (b) development roles. The analysis is illustrated by examples from national and local initiatives. Argues for a strengthening of teachers' role in both research and development.

183 HAVELOCK, R., 'The utilization of educational research and development' in HARRIS, A. *et al.*, (16) pp. 312–327

A very influential article which distinguishes three models for the utilization and dissemination of knowledge in education — the R.D. and D. model, the social interaction model, and the problem-solving model. These have been widely used in the analysis of curriculum change in Great Britain (See 9, 175 and 189).

184 HOLLY, D., *Beyond Curriculum*, Paladin, 1974

A Marxist critique of secondary education (characterized as 'alienated' and 'depersonalized'). Most curriculum development projects seen as essentially reaffirmations of the status quo. Well-written with some memorable phrases.

185 HOLT, M., *Schools and Curriculum Change*, McGraw Hill, 1980

An interesting summary discussion of curriculum change as it affects secondary education. Includes chapters on the context of change, the whole curriculum (the author's preoccupation!), managing the curriculum, examinations and accountability, 16–19 education, and strategies for curriculum change. Contains very useful summaries at the end of each chapter.

186 HOUSE, E., *The Politics of Educational Innovation*, McCutcheon, Berkeley, 1974

An important book dealing with aspects of the politics of innovation in USA. Valuable in the British context for its spatial analysis of innovation spread, for its stress on the importance of personal contacts in innovation diffusion and for its critique of R. and D. policy. Advocates a client-centred innovation system characterized by 'ecological gentleness'.

187 HOUSE, E., 'Technology versus craft: a ten year perspective on innovation', *J. Curriculum Studies*, 11:1, 1979, pp. 1–15.

A valuable overview. Argues that three perspectives ('technological', 'political' and 'cultural') have dominated thought on innovation during the last decade. Suggests there has been a shift in focus from innovation itself, to innovation-in-context, to context.

188 KING, E. (Ed.), *Reorganizing Education: Management and Participation for Change*, Sage, 1977

A very varied collection of articles on promoting and managing change in education including a useful paper on participation by Coombs, ones by Lawton and Chanan on reconceptualizing school curricula and one by Taylor on innovation without growth (198).

189 MACDONALD, B. and WALKER, R., *Changing the Curriculum*, Open Books, 1976

A challenging examination of curriculum development since 1960, with more general chapters being supplemented by detailed analyses of particular projects. Valuable chapters on 'Curriculum negotiation' and on 'Rhetoric and reality in curriculum renewal'.

190 MACLURE, S., *Styles of Curriculum Development*, OECD, Paris, 1972

An examination of 'style' in curriculum development. Although not coming to any definite characterization of different styles, the short book contains some interesting insights into contrasting styles of development in various countries. (See 179 an 197.)

191 NISBET, J., 'Innovation-bandwagon or hearse?' in HARRIS, A. et al. (16), pp. 1–14

After neatly discussing some of the inevitable problems associated with innovation in institutions, Nisbet argues for greater understanding of the dynamics of change and for structures which will enable institutions to be self-renewing. A surprisingly optimistic paper despite the title.

192 NYQUIST, E., 'Emerging strategies and structures for educational change in the United States' in *Emerging Strategies and Structures for Educational Change*, The Ontario Institute for Studies in Education, 1966

An extremely witty and insightful examination of educational change seen from the standpoint of the optimistic mid-sixties. Not easily accessible but well worth the effort of retrieval.

193 OWEN, J., *The Management of Curriculum Development*, Cambridge University Press, 1973

A curious book, failing to cohere overall, often unclear, yet containing many interesting observations most of which are not developed fully enough. Provides an overview of the English system of curriculum development and a valuable discussion of the future of development.

194 REID W. and WALKER, D., (Eds.), *Case-Studies in Curriculum Change: Great Britain and the United States*, Routledge and Kegan Paul, 1975

Features six case-studies with an editorial introduction to each and a concluding chapter discussing theories of curriculum design and diffusion. A valuable collection (more are needed like it), especially Walker's examination of curriculum deliberation in the Kettering Art Project and Hamilton's study of the 'implementation' of integrated science in two Scottish schools.

195 SCHON, D., *Beyond the Stable State*, Temple Smith, 1971

A widely quoted book which traces the implications of continuous social and economic change for the development of organizations. Especially valuable for its discussion of diffusion models which can be used to throw light on diffusion strategies. Well worth reading, though some of the detailed American examples can usefully be omitted. (See 175 and 183.)

196 SIEBER, S., 'Images of the practitioner and strategies of educational change', *Sociology of Education*, 45, 1972, pp. 362–385

Describes three change strategies each rooted in a particular image of the practitioner — the 'rational man', the 'cooperator' and the 'powerless functionary'. Suggests that each presents a useful perspective but none is complete in itself.

197 TAYLOR, P. and JOHNSON, M. (Eds.), *Curriculum Development: A Comparative Study*, Windsor, NFER, 1974

A collection of papers illustrating how curricula are developed in a sample of ten countries. The chapters examine the participants in the process, the kinds of decisions made, the way these are implemented and some of the forces impinging on the process. (See also 179.)

198 TAYLOR, W., 'Innovation without growth' *Ednl. Admin.*, 4:2, 1976 pp. 1–13

Describes the 'great bonanza' associated with educational expansion; argues there is no necessary link between innovation (equated with improvement) and growth, and suggests a number of staffing and resource strategies for facilitating innovation at a time when there is not likely be growth in 'real' terms.

199 WEBSTER, J., 'Curriculum change and "crisis"' *B.J. Ednl. Studies*, XXIV:3, Oct. 1976, pp. 203–218

Interesting discussion of the role of external events in creating educational discontinuities and with them the opportunity for curriculum change. Role of central government seen as 'the creation, when necessary, of crisis-making discontinuities'; the Schools Council viewed as a body with neither teeth nor crisis-making potential.

Project-based Development

200 BANKS, L., 'Curriculum developments in Britain 1963–68', *J. Curriculum Studies*, 1:3, Nov. 1969, pp. 247–259

A good article outlining the approach adopted by Schools Council with regard to its early curriculum development projects. The various stages in the development of curriculum materials are discussed.

201 EISNER, E., 'Curriculum development in Stanford University's Kettering Project: recollections and ruminations', *J. Curriculum Studies*, 7:1, May 1975, pp. 26–41

An account 'from the inside' of how the Kettering Art Project Team operated when developing their project materials. It is clear, readable and absorbing. For a more detailed analysis of their deliberations see Walker's paper (386).

202 GREIG, C. and REID, W., 'Proposals and possibilities in curriculum development: a study of the Cambridge School Classics Project', *J. Curriculum Studies*, 10:4 1978, pp. 329–348

With particular and detailed reference to the Cambridge School Classics Project, the authors argue that a persistent characteristic of national curriculum development projects has been the gap between the scale of work envisaged and the magnitude of the actual output. Criticizes the Schools Council for making no attempt to 'build up a bank of knowledge about problem definition, planning and management'. Poses the major question: were projects the appropriate response to all the major curriculum problems of the 60s and early 70s? (See also 107 and 23).

203 SCHOOLS COUNCIL, *Pattern and Variation in Curriculum Development Projects*, Macmillan, 1973

A short, useful account of various patterns of development adopted by sixteen English curriculum development projects. It explores why projects were set up, their aims, products and ways of working. The final chapter provides a number of interesting issues for consideration (See also 200).

204 SHIPMAN, M., *Inside a Curriculum Project*, Methuen, 1974

An interesting, at times fascinating, account of how the Keele Integrated Studies Project originated, developed and altered. It charts the differences in perception among those involved and it throws light on the relationships among project teams, local authorities, heads and class teachers. Also contains a paper by Jenkins in which he explores relationships between the project team and teachers through employing a series of metaphors.

205 SHIPMAN, M., 'Contrasting views of a curriculum project', *J. Curriculum Studies*, 4:2, Nov. 1972, pp. 145–153

Discusses the various definitions of the Integrated Studies project held by the project team itself, by teachers and by advisers. Charts how these changed during the trial period. 'The curriculum scene is a busy market place where bargains are struck between parties who interpret the contract through their particular circumstances.'

206 WALKER, D., 'A naturalistic model for curriculum development', *School Review*, 80, Nov. 1971, pp. 51–65

In contrast to models which prescribe for curriculum design (*e.g.* STENHOUSE 12 and TYLER 143), Walker presents a descriptive model based on how a project team actually operated. The concepts employed are very different e.g. 'platform', 'data', 'policy' and 'deliberation'. It is not an easy article to read but important nonetheless.

School-focussed Development

207 CERI, *Creativity of the School*, OECD, Paris, 1973

A collection of seminar papers focussing on schools' abilities to generate, adopt, adapt or reject innovations. British contributions include Kogan on administrative relationships between schools and other agencies and McMullen on organization and relationships within the school. (See also 208)

208 CERI, *School-based Curriculum Development*, OECD, Paris, 1979

Includes a useful theoretical section on the case for school-based curriculum development, followed by six case-studies including 'School-based Curriculum Development in England' by John Eggleston. (See also 207)

209 EGGLESTON, S.J., (Ed.), *School-Based Curriculum Development in Britain: A Collection of Case-Studies*, Routledge and Kegan Paul, 1980

A collection of essays related mainly to teacher-initiated developments in English secondary education. A useful, if over-confident, editorial introduction is followed by six case-studies which focus on the problems of support for, and organization of, school-based developments rather than on curricular decision-making itself. Overall, a modest contribution to a neglected area of curriculum research.

210 ELLIOTT, J. and ADELMAN, C., *Innovation at the Classroom Level*, E. 203, *Curriculum Design and Development*, unit 28, Open University Press, Milton Keynes, 1976

A description of the Ford Teaching Project designed to help teachers implement discovery/inquiry approaches in their classrooms. Describes how the researchers helped teachers clarify their thinking and helped them develop and test a number of generalizations about teaching strategies. An example of curriculum researchers in a consultancy role. Not always easy to follow but worth the effort.

211 EVANS, P. and GROARKE, M., 'An exercise in managing curriculum development in a primary school' in *Aims, Influence and Change in the Primary School Curriculum*, TAYLOR, P. (Ed.), Windsor, NFER, 1975, pp. 103–137

A detailed case-study focussing on the introduction of a new language programme in a primary school. Heartening to read of the success of the venture; most other case studies of schools deal with failures (see 366 and 380).

212 GOODLAD, J., 'Staff development: the league model' in HARRIS, A. *et al.* (16), pp. 143–153

Discusses the rationale and practice of the League of Cooperating Schools, an improvement strategy which focussed not on individual teachers but on the school as the organic unit for change and which linked such schools in a mutually supportive social system.

213 GOODSON, I., 'The teachers' curriculum and the new reformation, *J. Curriculum Studies*, 7:2, Nov. 1975, pp. 160–169

Based on experience of social studies teaching at Countesthorpe, Goodson argues for the impossibility of radical curriculum change while teachers' basic curricular assumptions remain intact. He outlines how despite modifications in classroom practice, the curriculum remained the teachers', not the pupils'.

214 GRAY, H., *Change and Management in Schools*, Nafferton, 1979

Contends that 'the task of management is the search for freedom and the making it real for everyone in the school'. Discusses 'Staff and organization development', 'Groups, teams and leadership', 'Changing the curriculum' and 'Principles of management'.

215 HARGREAVES, A., 'The rhetoric of school-centred innovation', *J. Curriculum Studies*, 14:3, 1982, pp. 251–266

Argues for critical understanding and discussion of school-centred innovation and suggests there is a particular lack of empirically grounded accounts of innovation in action. Helpfully reviews work in this area.

216 HENDERSON, E. and PERRY, G. (Eds.) *Change and Development in Schools*, McGraw-Hill, 1981

Contains an extended introduction on school-focussed inservice education and the change process, followed by twelve comparatively short case-studies dealing with change in a variety of educational settings. (But see 215)

217 HOLT, M., *The Common Curriculum*, Routledge and Kegan Paul, 1978

Provides a rationale for the comprehensive school curriculum and suggests how it can be organized to give all pupils an effective education which reflects a balanced view of our culture. Polemic in parts but well argued with reference to theoretical work in curriculum studies. (See also 218)

218 HOLT, M., *Regenerating the Curriculum*, Routledge and Kegan Paul, 1979

Discusses the secondary school curriculum in the light of the 'Great Debate' and its aftermath. Simply but effectively, it examines the implications of school-based development of the whole curriculum for national projects, for inservice training, for accountability, and for the management of change processes in the school.

219 HOYLE, E., 'The creativity of the school' in HARRIS, A. *et al.* (16), pp. 329–346

Examines the problem of institutionalizing innovations in English secondary schools. Outlines strategies of innovation (see 183) and discusses problems of authority, professionalism and support for teacher development. A useful overview of thinking about how to enable schools to sustain innovation. (See also 207)

220 HOYLE, E., *Strategies of Curriculum Change*, E. 203, *Curriculum Design and Development*, unit 23, Open University Press, Milton Keynes, 1976

A useful introduction to some of the concepts employed in discussions of curriculum change. It also summarizes the main features of strategies for organizational and curricular change, along with their advantages and disadvantages. (See also 178, 183, 196 and 219).

221 MILES, M., 'Planned change and organizational health: figure and ground' in HARRIS, A. *et al.* (16), pp. 192–203

Examines the concept of 'organizational health' which refers to an organization's ability not just to cope with change but to develop along desired lines. Proposes ten dimensions of such 'health' and six interventions aimed at improving it.

222 PRESCOTT, W., *School-based Curriculum Development* E. 203, *Curriculum Design and Development*, unit 26, Open University Press, Milton Keynes, 1976

Explores the strengths and weaknesses of the arguments in favour of school-based development. Three themes are emphasized: the role of the school and the teacher; the need for participation in decision-making; and the need for effective supporting agencies. (See 224 and 83)

223 SARASON, S., *The Culture of the School and the Problem of Change*, Allyn and Bacon, Boston, 1972

Argues that in education 'the more things change, the more they remain the same'. Locates the problem in the culture of the school which inhibits innovation.

224 SKILBECK, M., 'School-based curriculum development and teacher education' in PRESCOTT, W. (222)

Provides a well-argued rationale for school-based development, outlines objections to it and provides a design model for school use. Argues that it represents an ideology — a movement growing out of teacher autonomy and dissatisfaction with imposed curricula. (See also 83 and 222)

225 TAYLOR, P., *How Teachers Plan their Courses*, NFER, Windsor, 1970

A research report which traces the planning procedures adopted by a sample of secondary school teachers of geography, English and science. In his last chapter the author puts forward a model for curriculum planning based on his research.

226 WALKER, R. and MACDONALD, B., *Curriculum Innovation at School Level*, E. 203, *Curriculum Design and Development*, unit 27, Open University Press, Milton Keynes, 1976

Examines teachers' reactions to project-based development at secondary school level. Not easy reading, but faithfully reflects the conflicts and complexities of adoption/adaption activity. (See also 189 and 23)

227 WALTON, J. and WELTON, J. (Eds.), *Rational Curriculum Planning: Four Case Studies*, Ward Lock, 1976

Case-studies of change in a primary school, an emerging middle school, a comprehensive school and a college of education, examined from sociological and 'curriculum theory' perspectives. A wide view of 'rational planning' is taken, participants' descriptions are given, and editorial commentaries given on these. Useful, but does not quite come off as an analysis of the change process from which generalizations can be drawn.

Curriculum Dissemination, Adoption and Implementation

228 BERMAN, P. and MCLAUGHLIN, W., *Federal Programs Supporting Educational Change: Vol. IV. The Findings in Review*, Rand, Santa Monica, 1975

An overview of research findings focussing on the adoption of 29 projects in the United States but also surveying material from 293 projects. Main factors affecting innovation were the institutional setting (see 221), the implementation strategy adopted locally and the scope of change implied by the project relative to its setting.

229 BROWN, S., 'Key issues in the implementation of innovations in schools', *Curriculum*, 1:1, 1980, pp. 32–39

An article which summarizes the costs and benefits of innovation and which suggests how innovations and school contexts might be analyzed. Ends by suggesting eleven general principles to be taken into account in planning an innovation strategy. (See also 177 and 375)

230 COOPER, K., 'Curriculum diffusion: some concepts and their consequences', *Research Intelligence*, 3:1, 1977, pp. 6–7

Discusses the concepts of 'adoption', 'communication', 'implementation' and 'user-centred diffusion' and indicates how the use of these concepts has implications for action.

231 DOYLE, W. and PONDER, G., 'The practicality-ethic in teacher decision-making', *Interchange*, 8:3, 1977/78, pp. 1–12

Argues for the importance of the practicality ethic. Three general criteria appear to be used in deciding whether a curriculum proposal is 'practical': instrumentality, congruence with teachers' perceptions of their situation, and cost.

232 EICHOLZ, A. and ROGERS, E., 'Resistance to adoption of audio-visual aids by elementary school teachers', in MILES, M. (Ed.), *Innovation in Education*, Teachers College Press, New York 1964, pp. 299–316

An early, widely quoted study noted for its typology of forms of rejection.

233 ELLIOTT, J., 'Dissemination and related concepts' Interim Working Paper 1, *Progress in Learning Science Dissemination Study*, Schools Council Publications, 1977

A valuable paper analyzing concepts of diffusion, dissemination, adoption and implementation. From the analysis a typology of possible dissemination patterns is developed. Helps clarify thinking in a fairly 'muddy' area.

234 FULLAN, M., 'Overview of the innovative process and the user', *Interchange*, 3:2/3, 1972

Provides an extensive summary of models and approaches to innovation and suggests that in the American context no significant, effective educational change has occurred. Argues that the user needs involvement at all stages of the innovative process rather than simply being expected to adopt a programme developed elsewhere. (See 235 and 236)

235 FULLAN, M., 'Research into educational innovation', in GRAY, H. (Ed.), *The Management of Educational Institutions*, The Falmer Press, Lewes, 1982, pp. 245–61

Discusses current knowledge and directions in research on the implementation of educational innovations. An update in some senses of the review by FULLAN and POMFRET (236). Considers (i) what is implementation, (ii) what factors affect success or failure, (iii) principles and people in implementation, (iv) reflections on implementation research. (See also 234)

236 FULLAN, M. and POMFRET, A., 'Research on curriculum and instruction implementation', *Review of Educational Research*, 47:1, 1977, pp. 335–397

A very extensive review of North American research into defining and measuring implementation and into identifying specific determinants of implementation. The paper ends by discussing the implications of the review for policy. (See also 234 and 235)

237 GOODLAD, J., KLEIN, F. et al., *Looking Behind the Classroom Door*, Jones and Co., Worthington second edition, 1974

An interesting, though somewhat depressing, report into how far a large sample of American elementary schools have adopted a range of innovations. The researchers report little change and massive uniformity but propose remedies including getting schools to cooperate for self-improvement (see 212).

238 HARDING, J., 'Curriculum change: a model of teacher decision-making', *J. Curriculum Studies*, 10:4, 1978, pp. 351–55

An offshoot of the Curriculum Diffusion Research Project (239). From questionnaire responses and interviews, four dimensions emerged as relevant to decision-making about adoption: dissatisfaction, acceptability, relevance and feasibility.

239 KELLY, P. et al., *Curriculum Diffusion Research Report*, Centre for Science Education, Chelsea College, 1975

Discusses the methodology and findings of research investigating the diffusion of science projects through questionnaires, data from examining boards and case-studies. Stresses the very diverse patterns of dissemination activities and the consequent difficulty of drawing out generalizations.

240 MACDONALD, B. and RUDDUCK, J., 'Curriculum research and development projects: barriers to success', *B.J. Ednl. Psych*, 41:2, 1971, pp. 148–154

A widely quoted article outlining problems and resistance encountered in attempting to change school curricula. Examines the phenomenon of 'innovation without change' (see also 223). Clearly written and based on the authors' experience with the Humanities Curriculum Project.

241 RUDDUCK, J., *Dissemination of Innovation: The Humanities Curriculum Project*, Schools Council Working Paper 56, Evans/Methuen, 1976

An interesting, sensitively-portrayed case-study detailing the shaping and development of a dissemination strategy, problems in LEA responses, communications, training, support and the part played by various agencies. Contains a richness of detail too often lacking in descriptions of curriculum development activities. (See also 242 and 243)

242 RUDDUCK, J., 'Dissemination as the encounter of cultures', *Research Intelligence*, 3:1, 1977, pp. 3–5

Cultural encounters seen as central features of dissemination activities; such encounters involve communication, interpretation and accommodation between the cultures of disseminating and recipient groups. Dissemination of MACOS used as an exemplar. (See also 241 and 243)

243 RUDDUCK, J. and KELLY, P., *The Dissemination of Curriculum Development*, European Trend Reports on Educational Research, NFER, Windsor, 1976

An analysis of recent thinking and practice based on studies of dissemination in five European countries. In particular, the review chapter repays close study. (See also 241 and 242)

244 SCHOOLS COUNCIL, *Dissemination and Inservice Training*, Pamphlet 14, 1974

A document which outlines the Council's thinking on dissemination at a time when it was beginning to appraise its impact. Useful practical suggestions made and research possibilities suggested, but very fundamental questions not asked (see 107).

245 STEADMAN S., PARSONS, C. and SALTER, B., *Impact and Take-Up Project: A First Interim Report to the Programme Committee of the Schools Council*, Schools Council Publications, 1978

Reports primary teachers' familiarity with, and use of, Schools Council projects, based on a large postal survey and visits to a considerable number of schools. (See also 246)

246 STEADMAN, S., PARSONS, C. and SALTER, B., *Impact and Take-Up Project: A Second Interim Report to the Schools Council*, Schools Council Publications, 1980

Reports secondary school teachers' familiarity with, and use of, Schools Council projects, based on a postal survey of 251 secondary schools and visits to 34 schools. (See also 245)

247 WARING, M., 'The implementation of curriculum change in school science in England and Wales', *European Journal of Science Education*, 1:3, 1979, pp. 257–275

A useful overview of curriculum change dealing with diffusion and dissemination, implementation, barriers to change, and school-based research. Many points equally applicable to other subject areas than science.

248 WATSON, G., 'Resistance to Change', E. 283, *The Curriculum: Context, Design and Development*, supplementary material, Open University Press, Bletchley, 1972

Discusses two broad categories of resistance: resistance in personality and resistance in social systems. Makes twelve recommendations for coping with resistance and instituting change. A useful paper.

249 WHITEHEAD, D., *The Dissemination of Educational Innovations in Britain*, Hodder and Stoughton, 1980

Analyzes models and strategies for the dissemination of innovations, with particular reference to the Schools Council History, Geography and Social Science 8–13 Project. Predictable conclusions but a useful introduction to the area.

7 Curriculum Management

(compiled by Ken Shaw, School of Education, University of Exeter)

250 BECKETT, L., *Maintaining Choice in the Secondary Curriculum*, Centre for Educational Technology, 1981

Reports and discusses the results of a large investigation into the impact of falling rolls and associated managerial problems for secondary schools. Stresses the contribution of educational technology to the maintenance of a broad curricular offering through resource-based learning.

251 BLOOMER, M. and SHAW, K. (Eds.), *The Challenge of Educational Change*, Pergamon, Oxford, 1979

Reviews the organizational aspects of schooling as a context for curriculum delivery at primary and secondary level, with chapters specifically on curriculum management by Westbury and Seckington.

252 BRIAULT, E. and SMITH, F., *Falling Rolls in Secondary Schools*, NFER, Windsor, 1980

A detailed study of the curricular and organizational consequences of declining numbers supported by exemplary case studies. A fundamental contribution, rightly renowned.

253 BUSH, T. et al. (Eds.), *Approaches to School Management*, Harper and Row, 1980

Section V is one of the very few pieces of management writing which specifically confronts curriculum issues; there is much other relevant work in the book. It is attractively written.

254 DAUNT, P., *Comprehensive Values*, Heinemann Educational, 1975

Discusses the aims, modes, problems and policies as well as values of the comprehensive school. Is written by the practising head of a London school 'where the genuine pressures of a working situation compelled me to concentrate my ideas'. Not just how to manage but to what purpose.

255 DAWSON, P., *Making a Comprehensive Work*, Harper and Row, 1980

A toughminded no-nonsense account by a far from trendy head of another London school. Highly readable. Contentious or realistic according to taste.

256 DEPARTMENT of EDUCATION and SCIENCE/WELSH OFFICE, *Local Authority Arrangements for the School Curriculum*, HMSO, 1979

An analysis of responses to Circular 14/77 issued to collect information from LEAs about their policies and practices. Indicates the aspirations of central government and the responsibilities of the local authorities, and the possibility of general agreement about a framework within which a school curriculum may be managed.

257 HURMAN, A., *A Charter for Choice*, NFER, Windsor, 1978

Studies the organization and management of third year option schemes formally and informally in relation to ideas of balance and pupil choice in comprehensive schools and to the myths and processes on which this element in the curriculum rests.

258 WALTON, J. (Ed.), *The Secondary School Timetable*, Ward Lock Educational, 1972

Mistitled. In fact about the organizational context of curriculum planning and implementation: problems, case studies, planning for flexibility. Good technical treatment; clearly written discussions of how to go about it by practitioners.

259 WESTON, P., *Negotiating the Curriculum*, NFER, Windsor, 1979

A detailed case study of negotiating the curriculum amongst the different interest groups and the social system of the school. Much is at classroom level; much needed illustration of the process of curriculum decision-making in real conditions. Readable and realistic.

8 Curriculum Evaluation, Assessment and Accountability

260 ANDERSON, D., *Evaluating Curriculum Proposals*, Croom Helm, 1980

A strange, rather difficult book which suggests questions and methods for the critical analysis of curriculum texts. Examines the ways a number of texts are written so as to influence readers towards accepting their suggestions. A very different 'evaluation' text from the others in this section of the bibliography.

261 ASHTON, P. et al., *An Approach to Evaluation, The Pupils and the Curriculum, The Teacher and the Curriculum, Continuing Evaluation*, P. 234, *Curriculum in Action*, Blocks 1–4, Open University Press, Milton Keynes, 1980

A series of eight units providing detailed guidance on how teachers can observe what is happening in their classrooms, analyze their observations, judge the value of the data obtained, and use it to make further decisions. The units discuss six main questions: '1. What did the pupils actually do? 2. What were they learning? 3. How worthwhile was it? 4. What did I do? 5. What did I learn? 6. What do I intend to do now?' The questions and general principles are illustrated and elaborated by very many examples of classroom evaluation written by practising teachers.

262 ATKIN, M., 'Education accountability in the United States', *Educational Analysis*, 1:1, 1979, pp. 5–21

A keenly observed, well written account of some of the forms taken by the American accountability movement in the last twenty years and some of the latter's causes. Well complements MacDonald's analysis of accountability in England (295).

263 BECHER, T. and MACLURE, S. (Eds.), *Accountability in Education*, NFER, Windsor, 1978

An excellent collection of papers analyzing the concept of accountability, discussing present trends and providing pointers for future policy-making. The editors provide informative introductory and concluding pieces; other contributions of note include 'Procedures for assessment' (Nisbet), 'Accountability, standards and the process of schooling' (MacDonald) and 'An American view of British accountability' (House). (See also 264, 295, 298, 314 and 318)

264 BECHER, T. et al., *Policies for Educational Accountability*, Heinemann, 1981

A cogently argued analysis of accountability issues at school and LEA levels. Highly recommended as an analysis and for its practical suggestions re. policies for accountability. (See 263)

265 BLOOM, B., HASTINGS, J. and MADAUS, G., *Handbook on Formative and Summative Evaluation of Student Learning*, McGraw-Hill, New York, 1971

A massive compendium of material on evaluation based on the specification of behavioural objectives. There are general sections on the use of objectives and on evaluation techniques, and there are chapters dealing with particular areas of the curriculum including language arts, science, maths and art education. The book represents a very formidable tradition within the area of evaluation. Needs highly selective reading.

266 BROADFOOT, P., *Assessment, Schools and Society*, Methuen, 1979

A sociological analysis of the origins of school assessment, of international perspectives and trends, and of the ideology of assessment.

267 CHOPPIN, B., 'Educational measurement and the item bank model' in LACEY, C. and LAWTON, D. (Eds.) (292), pp. 204-221

Quite technical but an interesting defence of item-banking. Tackles the difficult question: 'How can educational measurement be achieved through item-banking, given that it is essentially a one-dimensional process that we need to apply in what is essentially a multi-dimensional situation?'

268 CRONBACH, L., 'Course improvement through evaluation', *Teachers College Record*, 64, 1963, pp. 672-83

Defines evaluation as the 'collection and use of information to make decisions about an educational program'. Distinguishes three types of decision for which evaluation data may be used: course improvement, decisions about individuals and administrative regulation. Measurement procedures will necessarily vary in relation to these types of decision. A seminal article, still widely quoted.

269 DEARDEN, R., 'The assessment of learning', *British Journal of Educational Studies*, Vol. XXVII No. 2, 1979, pp. 111–124

An interesting article which attempts to widen the discussion of assessment beyond the concerns of psychometricians by applying an epistemological perspective to assessment procedures.

270 DENNISON, W., 'The Assessment of Performance Unit- where is it leading?', *Durham and Newcastle Research Review*, VIII, 40, 1978, pp. 31–38

A cogent critique of the APU. Four possible explanations offered as to the intentions of the DES in setting up the unit. Argues that the APU could be 'a backdoor method of introducing a new, tighter, more uniform pattern of management control of the educational system'. (See 292)

271 EISNER, E., 'On the uses of educational connoiseurship and criticism for evaluating classroom life', *Teachers' College Record*, 78:3, 1977, pp. 345–358

Advocates a wider, 'more generous' concept of evaluation to supplement scientific procedures. Suggests that many classroom phenomena cannot be measured, only 'rendered.' It is this richness and this complexity to which educational connoiseurship addresses itself'. A refreshing perspective from the field of art criticism. Beautifully written but not easy to understand. (See 10 and 326)

272 EISNER, E., *The Educational Imagination: On the Design and Evaluation of School Programs*, Collier-Macmillan, 1979

An excellent account of one approach to qualitative evaluation. Describes in detail the forms and functions of educational connoiseurship and criticism (see 271) and provides examples of such criticism. Convincingly demonstrates the value of artistic forms of understanding and reflection in the evaluation of curricula. (But see 277)

273 ELLIOTT, J., 'The conditions of public accountability', *Cambridge J. Ed.*, 7:2, 1977, pp. 100–104

Concisely and neatly spells out the conditions implicit in notions of 'public accountability'. Argues that genuine accountability enhances rather than detracts from teacher autonomy.

274 ELLIOTT, J. et al., *School Accountability*, Grant McIntyre, 1981

A series of essays on topics arising out of case-studies conducted as part of the SSRC Cambridge Accountability Project. Deals with theoretical and practical issues concerned with school self-acounting eg. teachers' perspectives on school accountability, the nature of trust, the task of school governors, teachers and advisers.

275 ERAUT, M. et at., *The Analysis of Curriculum Materials*, University of Sussex Education Area, Brighton, 1975

Provides a comprehensive schema for the detailed analysis of curriculum materials; the first work of its kind to be published in this country. (See also 297)

276 ERAUT, M., 'Accountability and evaluation' in SIMON, B. and TAYLOR, W. (Eds.), *Education in the Eighties: The Central Issues*, Batsford, 1981

Distinguishes three forms of personal accountability ('moral', 'contractual' and 'professional') and outlines possible accountability procedures. Argues that 'the implementation of school self-accounting depends on teachers developing an extended professional role which is both less individualistic and more self-critical.' A concise overview of many of the issues discussed by the Sussex Accountability Project (see 264).

277 GIBSON, R., 'Curriculum criticism: misconceived theory, ill-advised practice', *Cambridge Journal of Education*, 11:3, 1981, pp. 190–210

Argues that the theory and practice of curriculum criticism (as illustrated by the work of Eisner, Jenkins and Willis) is 'deeply flawed' producing 'a rash of narcissistic, self-indulgent "research" or "evaluation" documents.' In particular he argues '(1) The assumption that the curriculum is a work of art, or can be treated as one, must be abandoned. (2) The limits of the analogy: literary criticism = curriculum criticism, must be more fully appreciated. In particular, prospective critics must respect the different natures, practices and functions of art and education.'

278 GOLDSTEIN, H., 'Limitations of the Rasch model for educational assessment' in LACEY, C. and LAWTON, D. (Eds.) (292) pp. 172–188

Discusses some of the limitations of the Rasch model and the implications of using the model for educational assessment. Suggests possible alternatives.

279 HALPIN, D., 'Exploring the secret garden', *Curriculum*, 1:2, Autumn 1980, pp. 32–45

An interesting, well-written critique of the HMI document, *Curriculum 11–16*. Stronger on criticisms than on suggestions as to how to improve the framework adopted by HMI. (See 393)

280 HALPIN, D., 'School-based curriculum review: what vocabulary should prevail?' *Curriculum*, 3:1, 1982, pp. 17–23

Argues that many LEA curriculum review documents focus on teachers' objectives rather than on the sorts of decisions teachers make when they attempt to operationalize their aspirations in the classroom. Such documents should help to increase teachers' understanding of how to implement more successfully the aspirations they already have, given the constraints of their particular school settings. An interesting discussion of 'the ambiguous, often messy, relationship between curricular ends and means'.

281 HAMILTON, D., *Curriculum Evaluation*, Open Books, 1976

A valuable straightforward account of the development of curriculum evaluation which discusses the various 'traditions' in the field and which is particularly interesting on the politics of evaluation and on its future.

282 HAMILTON, D. et al. (Eds.), *Beyond the Numbers Game*, Macmillan, 1977

A reader in 'illuminative evaluation', one of the 'traditions' discussed in 281. Its commentaries are both entertaining and memorable; the objectives model is 'revisited'; the work of five advocates of change is discussed; and an alternative evaluation methodology is proposed and illustrated. Some of the extracts are a little too short to do justice to the original papers, but the 'flavour' of the new approach comes over clearly.

283 HARLEN, W., *Science 5–13: A Formative Evaluation* Macmillan, 1975

A detailed 'insider's' account of the formative evaluation of the Science 5–13 Project. Especially interesting are the changes in evaluation strategy which developed as a result of experience with evaluating the early units.

284 HARLEN, W. (Ed.), *Evaluation and the Teacher's Role*, Schools Council Research Series, Macmillan, 1978

An interesting collection of essays, at varying levels of sophistication, written largely with teacher-readers in mind. Topics covered include evaluation and individual pupils (Harlen), classroom accountability and the self-monitoring teacher (Elliott), organization for learning (Hamilton) and evaluating the school as a whole (Jackson and Hayter).

285 HARLEN, W., 'Accountability that is of benefit to schools', *J. Curriculum Studies*, 11:4, 1979, pp. 287–97

Classifies accountability programmes in terms of (a) their focus of information (transactions or outcomes), and (b) the locus of control over information (internal or external to the schools). States that 'accountability measures are more likely to be fair and beneficial to schools, if the information comes from the schools and concerns transactions as well as outcomes.'

286 HARLEN, W. and ELLIOTT, J., 'A checklist for planning or reviewing an evaluation', in MCCORMICK, R. *et al.* (Eds.) (298), 1982, pp. 296–304

Provides a ten-point checklist for designing an in-school evaluation and a sixteen-point list for reviewing a report of such an evaluation.

287 HOLT, M., *Evaluating the Evaluators*, Hodder and Stoughton, 1981

A vitriolic attack on the Assessment of Performance Unit and on the fashionable trend towards self-evaluation in schools. Argues that improvement will come from improving the quality of curriculum deliberation and decision-making, not primarily from assessing outcomes — at either school or national levels.

288 HOUSE, E. (Ed.), *School Evaluation: The Politics and Process*, McCutcheon, Berkeley, 1973

A varied collection of readings almost entirely from American literature illustrating the thesis that 'evaluation is an integral part of the political processes of our society'. Decision-making, politics and the evaluation of teacher competence feature as prominent themes. Contains House's own paper; 'The conscience of educational evaluation'.

289 JENKINS, D., *Six Alternative Models of Curriculum Evaluation*, E. 203, *Curriculum Design and Development*, unit 20, Open University Press, Milton Keynes, 1976

Brief, tightly packed but valuable summary of approaches. Analyzes (and illustrates) six evaluation models in terms of key emphasis, purpose, key activities, key view point, outside experts needed, teaching staff involvement, risks and pay off. Small-scale parallel evaluation activities are suggested for the reader to pursue.

290 JENKINS, D., SIMONS, H. and WALKER, R., '"Thou nature art my goddess" Naturalistic inquiry in educational evaluation', *Cambridge Journal of Education*, 11:3, 1981, pp. 169–189

Summarizes discussions held at the third Cambridge workshop on the use of naturalistic methods in educational evaluation. In particular, it examines the promises and potential of naturalistic methods and addresses the problem of their relevance in policy contexts. (See also 282 and 354)

291 KEMMIS, S., 'Nomothetic and idiographic approaches to the evaluation of learning', *J. Curriculum Studies*, 10:1, 1978, pp. 45-59

Reviews recent developments in evaluation methodology including case-study and 'portrayal'. Argues that such recent approaches give little attention to the problem of evaluating pupils' learning. Advocates 'idiographic' methods of evaluation which provide descriptions of actual learning processes and outcomes.

292 LACEY, C. and LAWTON, D. (Eds.), *Issues in Evaluation and Accountability*, Methuen, 1981

A good selection of papers dealing with the methodology of curriculum evaluation (useful for research students in curriculum studies) and with the theoretical underpinning of the work of the Assessment of Performance Unit (of wider relevance). In relation to the latter topic, there are two particularly valuable papers: 'Monitoring performance: reflections on the Assessment of Performance Unit' (PRING) and 'Limitations of the Rasch model for educational assessment' (GOLDSTEIN).

293 LELLO, J. (Ed.), *Accountability in Education*, Ward Lock, 1979

A useful, though inevitably uneven collection of perspectives on accountability from contributors occupying very diverse roles within the education service. Contributors include an ex-Minister of State for Education, the Senior Chief Inspector, a CEO, an elected member, a parent, and teachers of varying levels of seniority. A very valuable chapter on 'The Accountability of HM Inspectorate (England)'. (See also 263)

294 MACDONALD, B., 'Who's afraid of evaluation?' *Education 3-13*, 4:2, 1976, pp. 87-91

A hard-hitting critique. Distinguishes between evaluation and assessment and discusses recent trends in England especially the preoccupation with 'efficiency' and 'standards'. Argues the DES is adopting an 'extremely rudimentary and simplistic' evaluation model and proposes democratic evaluation (see his paper in 322) as an alternative. (See also 295)

295 MACDONALD, B., 'Hard Times: educational accountability in England', *Educational Analysis*, 1:1, Summer 1979, pp. 23-43

An excellent socio-historical analysis of developments leading to demands for greater educational accountability in England. Many memorable phrases. A very insightful account.

296 MACINTOSH, H. et al., *Measuring Learning Outcomes*, P 234, *Curriculum in Action*, Block 6, Open University Press, Milton Keynes, 1981

The first two parts of the block discuss the purposes and limitations of assessment, and the content of assessment. Part three discusses various methods of assessment — standardised tests, school and class tests, and observing and recording children's progress. Part four discusses an assessment policy for the school related to the various audiences for whom assessments are made.

297 MCCORMICK, R., *Analysing Curriculum Materials*, P 234, *Curriculum in Action*, Block 7, Open University Press, Milton Keynes, 1981

Provides a framework for the analysis of school-produced materials, and (uncritically) introduces readers to the Sussex scheme for the analysis of published materials (275). Discusses the nature of curriculum materials analysis, particularly in relation to evaluation methodology and the issue of objectivity.

298 MCCORMICK, R. et al., *Calling Education to Account*, Heinemann, 1982

A collection of readings on accountability, strategies and techniques of evaluation (especially case-study and school self-evaluation), and reporting accounts and evaluations. A useful compilation with some previously unpublished material (see 286 and 320).

299 MCINTYRE, D., 'What responsibilities should teachers accept?', *Seminar Paper 1*, Department of Education, University of Stirling, 1977

Approaches the problem of accountability by examining five levels of criteria in terms of which teachers might accept responsibility for their teaching. Arguments are considered about the morality, and rationality, of accepting responsibility at each of these levels.

300 MUNROE, R., *Innovation: Success or Failure?*, Hodder and Stoughton, 1977

A critical examination of 'experimental' and 'illuminative' strategies of curriculum evaluation as practised in Britain up to the mid-seventies. Concludes that many evaluation studies failed to demonstrate their value for educational practice, mainly because of (a) confusion about the purpose of evaluation, and (b) 'an inability on the part of evaluators to relate the terms of their assessments to a recognizable world of classrooms and schools.'

301 PARLETT, M. and HAMILTON, D., 'Evaluation as Illumination: a new approach to the study of innovatory programmes', Centre for Research in Educational Sciences, *Occasional Paper 9*, University of Edinburgh

An important paper in the emergence in this country of new-style curriculum evaluation. Argues that evaluation should be more concerned with illuminating complex situations than with measuring products. (See 282 and 302)

302 PARSONS, C., 'The new evaluation: a cautionary note', *J. Curriculum Studies*, 8:2, 1976, pp. 125–138

A critique of the 'new' evaluation which outlines some of its weaknesses and asserts that 'our methods, concerns and conceptualizations can be viewed, to an extent, as cultural artefacts; such a perspective may be of value in maintaining a critical awareness of new orthodoxes'. (See 282 and 303)

303 PARSONS, C., 'A policy for educational evaluation' in LACEY, C. and LAWTON, D. (Eds.) (292), pp. 39–68

Characterizes much recent curriculum evaluation as merely 'information-gathering'. Argues that evaluation questions should be turned into research problems and pursued according to disciplinary values.

304 PRING, R., 'Monitoring performance: reflections on the APU', in LACEY, C. and LAWTON, D. (Eds.), (292), pp. 156–171

A balanced appraisal. Discusses four fundamental problems: (a) the unit's adoption of a particular curriculum model, (b) its focus on 'development', (c) the distinction it makes between form and content, and (d) its selection of objectives. Believes the unit has broken new and valuable ground with its conceptual mapping of curricular areas, its research into assessment techniques, and its use of item-banking.

305 SATTERLEY, D., *Assessment in Schools*, Blackwell, Oxford, 1981

An excellent introduction — well-conceived, clearly presented and interestingly written. Provides detailed guidance on assessment techniques teachers might use and also discusses theoretical and ideological issues concerned with the practice of assessment. Provides a particularly readable account of the Rasch method of objective measurement used by the APU in its attempts to monitor national levels of achievement over time.

306 SCHOOLS COUNCIL, *Evaluation in Curriculum Development: Twelve Case-studies*, Macmillan, 1973

A very varied collection of papers dealing with the evaluation approaches adopted by a variety of Schools Council projects. For contrasting approaches see the papers by Kelly, Harlen, MacDonald and Jenkins. (See also 322)

307 SCRIMSHAW, P., 'Illuminative evaluation: some reflections', *Journal of Further and Higher Education*, 3:2, Spring 1979, pp. 35–43

Outlines features of a number of 'illuminative' approaches, which are classified into three types: 'honest broker', 'external expert', and 'joint evaluation'. Believes that more published accounts using specific kinds of illuminative methods and a comparative study of their strengths and weaknesses are needed.

308 SCRIVEN, M., 'The methodology of evaluation', in TYLER R. et al, *Perspectives of Curriculum Evaluation* (323), pp. 39–83

A widely quoted article tracing a number of crucial distinctions in evaluation e.g. goals versus roles of evaluation, formative versus summative evaluation, evaluation studies versus process studies, 'intrinsic' evaluation versus 'pay-off' evaluation. The article itself has been a 'formative' influence in this developing area.

309 SCRIVEN, M., 'Pro's and con's about goal-free evaluation', *Evaluation Comment*, 3:4, 1972, pp. 1–4

Distinguishes between internal and external evaluation of development activities. Argues that explicit goals are needed for planning, development and internal evaluation, but that external evaluation should examine the whole range of actual effects, especially unanticipated consequences. In this sense external evaluation would be 'goal-free'. (See 289)

310 SHIPMAN, M., *In-School Evaluation*, Heinemann, 1979

Relates the assessment of schools' effectiveness to moves towards more open schooling and argues that 'The right to autonomy rests on the duty to evaluate.' Describes how secondary schools can undertake assessment programmes (both internally and externally referenced) and considers the evaluation of other aspects of school life and organisation. Ruefully remarks that 'The contribution of the academic world to the evaluation of everyday, routine schooling has been negligible'; the book helps remedy that deficiency.

311 SIMONS, H., 'Process evaluation in schools', in LACEY, C. and LAWTON, D. (Eds.) (292), pp. 114-144

Discusses the methodology of process evaluation and process evaluation in practice in schools. Argues that (a) process evaluation should be a continuing aspect of professional practice, (b) it needs to be separated for a time from accountability demands, and (c) in the long term it may lead to a form of accountability consistent with professionalism.

312 SMETHERHAM, D. (Ed.), *Practising Evaluation*, Nafferton, 1981

A discussion of methodological and epistemological issues in evaluation raised by ten contributors, all of who have been engaged in the enterprise. Contributors include Dean ('Evaluation and advisers'), Shipman ('Parvenu Evaluation') and Walker ('On the uses of fiction in educational research').

313 SOCKETT, H., 'Teacher Accountability', *Phil. of Ed. Soc. Proc.*, vol. X, pp. 34-57, 1976

Usefully distinguishes two kinds of accountability: accountability based on the achievement of results and that based on principles governing practice. Provides a critique of the first and arguments to support the second. (See also 299 and 314)

314 SOCKETT, H. (Ed.), *Accountability in the English Educational System*, Hodder and Stoughton, 1980

A useful collection of papers by philosophers interested in conceptual and policy issues related to accountability. A clear analysis of contemporary issues by the editor is followed by a number of papers including 'Should schools determine their own curricula?' (White), 'Accountability and the politics of the staffroom' (Bridges) and 'The autonomous teacher' (Bailey).

315 STAKE, R., 'The countenance of educational evaluation', *Teachers College Record*, 68:7, 1967, pp. 523-40

A significant paper which analyzes the many facets of evaluation including the consideration of intents and observations, the making of judgements and the use of three bodies of data: antecedents, transactions and outcomes. Widely referred to (see 289).

316 STAKE, R., *Evaluating Educational Programmes: the need and the response*, OECD, Paris, 1976

A valuable summary of evaluation thinking and practice. Discusses the various responses made by government officials, educationists and researchers to the need for evaluation, analyses nine evaluation approaches and discusses the vexed problem of negotiating agreements to do evaluation studies. A very useful bibliography provided.

317 STEADMAN, S., 'Evaluation techniques' in MCCORMICK, R. et al (Eds.), (298), pp. 211-223

Discusses a range of techniques of direct use to schools engaged in self-evaluation.

318 STENHOUSE, L., 'Accountability', *Educatinal Analysis*, 1:1, 1979

An issue devoted entirely to accountability and providing a fascinating variety of perspectives from those directly or indirectly involved in accountability pressures. Particularly interesting papers from ATKIN (262), MACDONALD (295), Stenhouse ('Accounts of two kinds'), Dahloff ('The classroom complexities behind the test scores: some Swedish experience') and Rand ('Accountability and resistance: the Norwegian teaching profession under the Occupation').

319 STENHOUSE, L., 'The problem of standards in illuminative research', *Scottish Ednl. Studies*, 11:1, 1979, pp. 5-10

History is seen as a useful model on which to build an illuminative tradition which faces the problems of verification and accumulation. Argues that the issue in evaluation 'is not qualitative versus quantitative, but samples versus cases, and results versus judgements'.

320 STENHOUSE, L., 'The conduct, analysis and reporting of case-study in educational research and evaluation' in MCCORMICK, R. et al. (Eds.) (298), pp. 261-273

A previously unpublished paper which focuses on problems in analyzing and reporting case study data, emphasizing the parallels with historical research. Distinguishes between narrative, vignette and analysis as forms of presentation of case study results. Argues for interpretative descriptive case study which 'aims to strengthen judgement and develop prudence.'

321 STRAUGHAN, R. and WRIGLEY, J. (Eds.), *Values and Evaluation in Education*, Harper and Row, 1980

Discusses a number of important concepts — 'standards', 'measurement', 'evaluation' and 'values'. Discusses how questions about values and evaluation arise within the teaching of language, literature, art, history, science and mathematics.

322 TAWNEY, D. (Ed.), *Curriculum Evaluation Today: Trends and Implications*, Macmillan, 1975

A second volume to complement the Schools Council's first on evaluation (306). Considers a number of general issues, including changes in evaluation strategies over time (Harlen), the political use of evaluation studies (MacDonald) and a summary of research techniques used in evaluation studies (Steadman).

323 TYLER, R. et al., *Perspectives of Curriculum Evaluation*, AERA Monograph Series on Curriculum Evaluation 1, Rand McNally, Chicago, 1967

The first in a series of monographs on evaluation as practised in the United States. Contains papers by Tyler on changing concepts, by Gagné on curriculum research and the promotion of learning (including material on curriculum hierarchies) and an important paper by Scriven (308). Has a useful introductory piece by Stake (see also 315, and 316).

324 WHITE, J., 'The concept of curriculum evaluation' *J. Curriculum Studies*, 3:2, 1971, pp. 101–12

Valuably distinguishes various types of evaluation: that concerned with the efficiency of curricula in meeting stated ends, that concerned with comparing curricula, that concerned with the value of objectives being pursued and that involving the internal logic and consistency of curriculum plans. Helps clarify thinking in this difficult area.

325 WILLIS, G., 'Curriculum criticism and literary criticism', *J. Curriculum Studies*, 7:1, 1975, pp. 3–17

Develops further the views of Mann on curriculum criticism. Argues that a curriculum shares the same functions as a work of art and therefore an aesthetic perspective is essential to a comprehensive view of curriculum as a theoretical discipline and a practical art. See articles by MANN and WILLIS in 341.

326 WILLIS, G. (Ed.), *Qualitative Evaluation*, McCutcheon, Berkeley, 1978

A reader with a number of significant practical and theoretical examples of qualitative approaches to curriculum evaluation. Almost entirely North American in origin.

327 WISEMAN, S. and PIDGEON, D., *Curriculum Evaluation*, NFER, Windsor, 1970

A straightforward account of evaluation based on the specification of objectives and the use of instruments to measure their attainment. In the light of later thinking, it appears simplistic and narrow. Can serve as a layman's guide to BLOOM *et al.* (265)

9 Curriculum 'Theory' and Research

Curriculum 'Theory'

328 BEAUCHAMP, G., *Curriculum Theory*, (third edition), Kagg Press, Wilmette, 1975

Distinguishes three meanings to curriculum: as a written document, as a sub-system of schooling and as a field of study. Drawing almost entirely on American material, it discusses theory building, curriculum theory, values, curriculum design, curriculum engineering and curriculum as a field of study. Concludes with the nucleus of the author's own curriculum theory.

329 EGAN, K., 'Some presuppositions that determine curriculum decisions', *J. Curriculum Studies*, 10:2, 1978, pp. 123–133

Suggests that arguments about the curriculum are often arguments about pre-suppositions. The pre-suppositions examined include (i) human nature, good or bad?, (ii) culture, within or without?, (iii) consciousness, past, present, future?, (iv) centre of value, body, mind, soul? Believes that recognition of differing pre-suppositions might enable us to be more tolerant of disagreements and enable us to focus more precisely on those areas where we might work towards resolving disagreements.

330 EGAN, K., 'On the possibility of theories of educational practice', *J. Curriculum Studies*, 14:2, 1982, pp. 153–165

Contends that in deriving theories of educational practice, work should first focus on the data of children's interests and their typical ways of making sense of the world and their experience. Outlines three stages through which children pass: 'the mythic', 'the romantic', and 'the philosophic'. Believes that curriculum-making should be in tune with these stages. Warns against current 'psychologized' educational research: 'It is far from clear that educational research has any better tools than observation, memory and the fashioning of good reasons.'

331 EISNER, E., 'Humanistic trends and the curriculum field', *J. Curriculum Studies*, 10:3, 1978, pp. 197–204

Discusses the origins and uses of 'qualitative forms of enquiry' as a counterweight to more scientific, 'reductionist' approaches. Confesses that qualitative methods are demanding, the time it takes to use them exceptionally long, the questions of generalisability difficult, and the verification of their conclusions complex.

332 GOLBY, M., 'Practice and theory', in LAWN, M. and BARTON, L. (Eds.) (337), pp. 216–236

An interesting, partly auto-biographical examination of the relation of theory to practice in curriculum studies.

333 GRUMET, M., 'Restitution and reconstruction of educational experience: an autobiographical method for curriculum theory', in LAWN, M. and BARTON, L. (Eds.) (337), pp. 115–130

Describes none too clearly a rationale for the use of autobiography as a form of curriculum enquiry.

334 JENKINS, D., *The Current Debate*, E. 283, *The Curriculum: Context, Design and Development*, Open University Press, Bletchley, 1972

Discusses some of the uncertainties involved in curriculum study especially conflicts over theories and practices and over models and meanings. Provides commentaries on material by SCHWAB (347) LEACH on model-making, KING and BROWNELL (130) and JENKINS himself (where he discusses 'romantic' and 'classic' approaches to curriculum design). Not for the beginning student.

335 JENKINS, D., 'The moving plates of curriculum theory: a speculator's guide to future eruptions' in TAYLOR and WALTON (Eds.), (25), pp. 81–87

An amusing and splendidly irreverent look at possible developments in areas of curriculum study such as model-building, epistemology, the study of learning contexts and curriculum evaluation.

336 JOHNSON, M., 'The translation of curriculum into instruction', *J. Curriculum Studies*, 1:2, 1969, pp. 115–131

An example of a systems approach to curriculum study. Curriculum is seen as a structured series of learning outcomes which are the result of a curriculum development process and which constitute only one sub-system of the larger system for translating cultural content into individual learnings.

337 LAWN, M. and BARTON, L. (Eds.), *Rethinking Curriculum Studies*, Croom Helm

An interesting collection which attempts to reappraise, largely from a radical viewpoint, the field of curriculum studies in the UK and USA. Includes important papers by a number of theorists who have helped redefine the field in various ways *e.g.* PINAR and GRUMET's 'Theory and Practice in the Reconceptualisation of Curriculum Studies' (344) and REID's 'The Deliberative Approach to the Study of the Curriculum and its Relation to Critical Pluralism' (346). The book faithfully reflects the soul-searching and lack of coherence in this area of educational studies.

338 O'KEEFE, D., 'Towards a socio-economy of the curriculum', *J. Curriculum Studies*, 9:2, 1977, pp. 101–109

Examines the curriculum in terms of economic sociology. A difficult paper which argues that 'the curriculum expresses investment, consumption, and sub-systemic control activity in varying degrees of urgency, specificity and fusion'. Contends that the behaviour of the curriculum challenges the currently fashionable Marxist view of education as the relatively passive agency of the corporate state.

339 ORAM, R., 'An action frame of reference as a register for curriculum discourse', *J. Curriculum Studies*, 10:2, 1978, pp. 135–149

Proposes an enactment metaphor which sees curriculum, like a play, as a series of creations and re-creations. 'Curriculum enactment proposes that the curriculum be seen not as a process of development, diffusion and implementation but as what Escarpit called "creative treason", whereby authors' conceptions and intentions are deliberately and legitimately distorted, reinterpreted to make the work of art carry significant meanings to different people in different settings and at different times.'

340 PINAR, W. (Ed.), *Heightened Consciousness, Cultural Revolution and Curriculum Theory*, McCutcheon, Berkeley, 1974

A series of conference papers attempting to derive new directions for curriculum theory in the United States. Contains articles on ideologies, the politics of curriculum, existentialist philosophy, and the relevance of an emerging 'cultural revolution' for curriculum theory, An interesting but uneven collection. (See also 341)

341 PINAR, W. (Ed.), *Curriculum Theorising: The Reconceptualists*, McCutcheon, Berkeley, 1975

Presents a large number of articles by contemporary American theorists seeking to redefine and reconceptualize the curriculum field in directions far removed from those of TYLER (143) and TABA (8). Existentialist philosophy, phenomenological sociology and literary criticism are some of the perspectives applied. A fascinating, eclectic collection. (See also 340 and 337)

342 PINAR, W., 'The reconceptualisation of curriculum studies', *J. Curriculum Studies*, 10:3, 1978, pp. 205-214

Discusses three groups within the field of curriculum studies: 'traditionalists' (eg Tyler), 'conceptual-empiricists' (eg Westbury, Walker) and 'reconceptualists' who are concerned with 'a fundamental reconceptualisation of what curriculum is, how it functions and how it might function in emancipatory ways'. (See 341)

343 PINAR, W. and GRUMET, M., *Towards a Poor Curriculum*, Kendall/Hunt, Dubuque, 1976

An exploration of the curriculum as lived educational experience. An attempt to reconceptualize the study of the curriculum in terms of psychoanalytic, existential and phenomenological concepts. (See 344)

344 PINAR, W. and GRUMET, M. 'Theory and practice and the reconceptualisation of curriculum studies', in LAWN, M. and BARTON, L. (Eds.) (337), pp. 20-42

An interesting, though partial, account of developments in curriculum in the United States including an analysis of reconceptualization. (See 342 and 343)

345 REID, W., *Thinking about the Curriculum*, Routledge and Kegan Paul, 1978

The only English book yet published which examines in depth the nature of theorizing about the curriculum. Not easy reading but well worth consulting. A seminal contribution to the field.

346 REID, W., 'The deliberative approach to the study of the curriculum and its relation to critical pluralism', in LAWN, M. and BARTON, L. (Eds.) (337), pp. 160-187

An important paper despite its off-putting title. Describes a four-fold classification of approaches to the study of the curriculum — 'systemic', 'radical', 'existential', and 'deliberative' perspectives. Discusses in more detail the 'deliberative' approach. (See also 345)

347 SCHWAB, J., 'The practical: a language for the curriculum', *School Review*, 78:1, 1969, pp. 11-23

A plea for new perspectives on curriculum problems, Criticizes an over-theoretical approach and asks for a return to the practical to underpin better theory. A seminal paper. (See 334 and 348-9)

348 SCHWAB, J., 'The practical: arts of the eclectic', *School Review*, 79, 1971, pp. 493-542

Argues that curriculum needs to foster the arts of the eclectic i.e. to combine various behavioural sciences and to combine the different facets within any one science in order to meet practical problems. The complex problems of curriculum need polyfocal treatment. A difficult but challenging paper. (See also 347 and 349)

349 SCHWAB, J., 'The practical 3: translation into curriculum', *School Review*, 81, 1973, pp. 501-22

Outlines a planning strategy for translating scholarly material into curriculum material. Clear and well argued. (See also 347 and 348)

350 SHAW, K., 'Paradigms or contested concepts?', *British Journal of Educational Technology*, 7:2, 1976, pp. 18-23

Discusses curriculum studies' pre-occupation with the objectives paradigm. Argues that curriculum is 'a social matter. It is a matter of choices-in-the-situation, not rational-deductive prescriptions'. The field is characterised by 'contested concepts' — concepts variously interpreted by different groups and serving particular functions for groups.

351 SIMON, B. 'Problems in contemporary educational theory: a Marxist approach', *Journal of Philosophy of Education*, 12, 1978, pp. 29-39

A clear, beautifully written piece which sets out a Marxist orientation to certain major theoretical issues Emphasizes the importance of curriculum and pedagogy: 'The great perennial questions in education seem to me to be three.... What should be taught? To whom? How?'

352 SIMON, B., 'Why no pedagogy in England?', in SIMON, B. and TAYLOR, W. (Eds.), *Education in the Eighties: The Central Issues*, Batsford, 1981, pp. 124-145

A provocative paper which provides reasons for the neglect of pedagogy historically and which maintains that renewed attention should be paid to it. Argues that psychological knowledge combined with logical analysis of areas of knowledge forms the ground base from which pedagogical principles can be established, given effective research and experiment.

353 WESTBURY, I and WILKOF, N. (Eds.), *Science, Curriculum and Liberal Education: Selected Essays*, University of Chicago Press, Chicago, 1978

A collection of Joseph Schwab's essays concerned with 'What is a liberal education and what part can science play in it'; 'How should we think about the task of developing a curriculum?' 'How should educational research conceive of its goals?' An editorial introduction puts the essays into perspective and evaluates their significance. (See 347-9)

Curriculum Research

354 ADELMAN, C. et al., 'Re-thinking case-study: notes from the second Cambridge conference', *Cambridge J. Ed.*, 6:3, 1976, pp. 139-150

A non-technical account clarifying what case-study research is, outlining its methodology and discussing its possible advantages. It's seen as part of an historical/interpretative (rather than scientific) tradition. For a more detailed technical account. (See 290 and 377)

355 ASHTON, P. et al., *The Aims of Primary Education: A Study of Teachers' Opinions*, Macmillan, 1975

An example of a large-scale empirical study into teachers' opinions of the aims of primary education. Study based on an extensive qestionnaire carefully developed as a result of cooperation between the project team and participating teachers.

356 BARNES, D., *From Communication to Curriculum*, Penguin, Harmondsworth, 1976

A different style of curriculum research which, based on transcripted conversations in classrooms, analyzes the different styles of discourse used, distinguishes two views of teaching and learning ('transmission' and 'interpretation') and examines the consequences for pupils. Usefully draws together material from curriculum studies, sociology of education and language research.

357 BARNES, D., 'Between all the stools: some methodological considerations in curriculum research', *J. Curriculum Studies*, 13:4, 1981, pp. 305-312

Discusses (a) researchers' motives for involving themselves in curriculum research, and (b) a range of methodologies used in curriculum research. Discusses both in relation to his own work. Argues that 'Researchers into the curriculum are in the business of forming opinions.... Curriculum research will not build up a systematic body of knowledge, partly because many of the underlying problems are ethical rather than technical, and partly because the nature of curriculum-its dependence upon the formation of meanings through contingent interaction — does not lead to "definitive" concepts and firm conclusions.'

358 BERLAK, A. and H., *Dilemmas of Schooling: Teaching and Social Change*, Methuen, 1981

Provides a theoretical perspective for examining teaching in the form of sixteen 'dilemmas' and illustrates these with reference to keenly observed incidents in a number of British primary schools. Goes on rather more uncertainly and less valuably to relate the 'dilemma language' to more general political, social and cultural issues.

359 BROUDY, H., 'Components and constraints of curriculum research', *Curriculum Theory Network*, Spring 1970, pp. 16–31

Argues that 'on the criteria of plenty and variety, curriculum research must be judged successful. On the more rigorous criteria of progress and the degree to which we are achieving a unified theory in terms of which generalizations can be accredited or discredited, curriculum reasearch has not been impressive.'

360 BURSTALL, C. et al., *Primary French in the Balance*, NFER, Windsor, 1974

An example of a particular kind of curriculum evaluation. A detailed evaluation, taking ten years, into the teaching of French in primary schools. Discusses in detail the methodology employed in assessing pupils' attitudes and attainments and the results obtained (including the researcher's judgement of their implications).

361 BYNNER, J., *Issues in Methodology*, P 234, *Curriculum in Action*, Open University Press, Milton Keynes, 1981

Relates evaluation in the classroom to basic principles and strategies of social science enquiry. Deals with some of the main principles of curriculum research and evaluation, including topics such as sampling, observations/measurements, analysis, and experimental versus illuminative approaches to evaluation.

362 CHEVERST, W., 'The role of the metaphor in educational thought: an essay in content analysis', *J. Curriculum Studies*, 4:1, 1972, pp. 71–82

A small-scale study involving the content analysis of major official publications on primary education and discussing the changing incidence and power of metaphors used this century.

363 DOCKRELL, W. and HAMILTON, D. (Eds.), *Rethinking Educational Research*, Hodder and Stoughton, 1980

A collection of papers on new directions in educational research pioneered in the 70s. Includes contributions on 'Research into practice' (Becher), 'Program Evaluation' (Stake) and 'Schooling as an agency of education: some implications for curriculum theory' (Westbury).

364 ELLIOTT, J., 'What is action-research in schools?', *J. Curriculum Studies*, 10:4, 1978, pp. 355-357

A usefully compact account which distinguishes three modes within the domain of practical reflection: action-research, deliberative mode, evaluative mode. Concentrates on discussing action-research as developed at CARE and the Cambridge Institute.

365 ELLIOTT, J. ADELMAN, C. et al., *Ford Teaching Project*, various units, Centre for Applied Research in Education, Norwich, 1975

A series of publications from the Ford Teaching Project discussing the theoretical bases of the action research conducted and giving examples of the classroom research procedures in action. Written by both researchers and participating teachers. An example of the kind of partnership advocated by STENHOUSE (12).

366 GROSS, N. et al., *Implementing Organizational Innovations*, Harper and Row, New York, 1971

A detailed sociological case-study of the attempted implementation of an innovative style of teaching in an American elementary school. Explains the reasons for its failure and draws implications for theories of innovation adoption and rejection. Has itself been criticized (69).

367 HEGARTY, E., 'The problem identification phase of curriculum deliberation: use of the nominal group technique', *J. Curriculum Studies*, 9:1, 1977, pp. 31-42

Focuses on how curriculum problems can be identified by a review group. Suggests criteria from selecting group members and puts forward a case for using 'nominal' group techniques for structuring group processes.

368 HOLT, M. 'Whole curriculum planning in schools: some research implications', *J. Curriculum Studies*, 14:3, 1982, pp. 267-276

Distinguishes three types of curriculum research: 'concept research', 'heuristic' or task-oriented research, 'mechanistic' research (especially classroom interaction). What is needed is 'an eclectic, naturalistic and wide-ranging style of inquiry which draws its dynamic from a study of curriculum process'.

369 JACKSON, P., *Life in Classrooms*, Holt-Rinehart, New York, 1968

A pioneering study of life as experienced in elementary school classrooms by both pupils and teachers. The 'hidden' curriculum of the schools is insightfully analyzed and beautifully rendered in print. The problems teachers face in adopting theoretical prescriptions for planning and evaluation in the light of classroom exigencies are highlighted.

370 HURMAN, A., *A Charter for Choice*, NFER, 1979

See (257).

371 MACDONALD, B. and WALKER, R., *Changing the Curriculum*, Open Books, 1976

The second half of the book contains a number of case-studies of projects developed as a result of the authors' research into the fate of selected secondary projects in schools. This SAFARI research is also reported in 226.

372 MIDDLETON, D., *Observing Classroom Processes*, P 234, *Curriculum In Action*, Block 5, Open University Press, Milton Keynes, 1981

Considers the general approaches and techniques needed to carry out systematic investigations of classroom processes e.g. audio-recording, video-recording, photography, observation schedules. The general points are illustrated by reference to a case-study of teachers in a community college. Contains a short section on general methodological issues such as the role of teacher as evaluator.

373 NIXON, J. (Ed.), *A Teacher's Guide to Action Research*, Grant McIntyre, 1981

Eight accounts by teachers and others of teacher-conducted research. Contains particularly interesting pieces by Shostak (on the role of teachers' centres in fostering this sort of research) and Verrier (on consultancy).

374 OLSON, J., 'Teacher constructs and curriculum change', *J. Curriculum Studies*, 12:1, 1980, pp. 1–11

Argues for the importance of constructs used by teachers to minimise ambiguity consequent on the diffuseness of their role. Part of the problem of curriculum change is the challenge of new proposals to familiar and unexamined constructs.

375 OLSON, J. (Ed.), *Innovation in the Science Curriculum*, Croom Helm, 1982

A lengthy editorial introduction precedes four case studies which deal with (a) the demands of activity-based science, (b) the costs and rewards of innovation from the teachers' viewpoint, (c) how teachers cope with inquiry teaching, and (d) a methodological commentary on a case-study of science education. The studies are 'sources for a better understanding of the process of change itself: how teachers cope with innovation; how they cope every day; and how outsiders might better appreciate life in schools, and the demands that new ideas make on the stable systems that allow teachers to cope.'

376 REID, W., 'What is curriculum research?', in TAYLOR, P. and WALTON, J. (Eds.) (25), pp. 90–98

Outlines the development of curriculum as a field of study, distinguishes curriculum research from curriculum development and outlines the scope of curriculum research using Stake's model (315). Justification for research seen in its provision of data relevant to policy-making. The move towards 'a naturalistic, humanistic, impressionistic mode of research' is predicted. (See also 345).

377 SAFARI, *Innovation, Evaluation, Research and the Problem of Control: Some Interim Papers*, CARE, Norwich, 1974

Discusses in detail a framework of rules and procedures for the conduct of case-study research. Also contains MacDonald's article, 'Evaluation and the control of education' (also published in 322) and a philosophical critique of SAFARI 'theory'. (See also 354)

378 SHAW, K., 'Understanding the curriculum: the approach through case-studies', *J. Curriculum Studies*, 10:1, 1978, pp. 1–17

A useful overview of case-study approaches. Three types of study are isolated and examples described: (a) descriptive studies (*e.g.* those in WALTON and WELTON (227)), (b) analytical studies (*e.g.* DICKINSON 119), (c) studies of deliberation (*e.g.* SHIPMAN (204)).

379 SHIPMAN, M., *Inside a Curriculum Project*, Methuen, 1974

One of the few easily accessible and readable case-studies dealing with the development of a particular curriculum project. Comments on the researcher's own role and activities are given by members of the project team.

380 SMITH, L. and KEITH, P., *Anatomy of Educational Innovation*, Wiley, New York, 1971

An indepth examination of a would-be innovative American elementary school. Employs anthropological/ethnographic research techniques which provide a useful contrast to the approach used by GROSS et al., (366).

381 STENHOUSE, L., (12) chapters 9 and 10.

Argues that with the help of educationists in a consultancy role, teachers can research into their own problems and test their hypotheses in the classroom situation. Gives, none too convincingly, examples of the kind of classroom research he advocates.

382 STENHOUSE, L., 'Curriculum research and the art of the teacher', *Curriculum*, 1:1, 1980, pp. 40-44

A beautifully written, occasionally elliptic paper. Makes two central claims: (a) 'the expression of educational ideas in curricular form provides a medium for the development — and, if necessary, the autonomous self-development — of the teacher as artist' (b) 'The improvement of schooling through curriculum research and development is about the improvement of the art of the teacher. It is not about the improvement of students' learning outcomes *without* improving the art of teaching'.

383 TAYLOR, P., REID, W. and HOLLEY, B., *The English Sixth Form: a case study in curriculum research*, Routledge and Kegan Paul, 1974

Outlines one perspective on the scope of curriculum studies and research. Exemplifies this in a detailed examination of the sixth form curriculum. Topics examined include aims and objectives, influences and constraints, the role of universities and the importance of the organisational context.

384 TAYLOR, P. and RICHARDS, C., (9), chapter 8

Distinguishes between prescriptive and 'scientific' curriculum theory and outlines broad areas of research (illustrated by examples) which can help contribute to the 'scientific' study of the curriculum.

385 WALKER, D., 'What curriculum research?', *J. Curriculum Studies*, 5:1, 1973, pp. 58-72

A well-written critique of the failure of curriculum to clarify the nature of the phenomena and the problems it addresses. Argues this failure is due in part to misconceptions as to the nature and aims of empirical research into a field concerned with practice. (See also 347 and 381)

386 WALKER, D., 'Curriculum development in an art project', in REID, W. and WALKER, D. (Eds.) (194), p. 91-135

An excellent analysis of the internal deliberations of the Kettering Art

Project team. Draws on his naturalistic model for curriculum development (206) and compares the actual way the team operated as opposed to the procedures enshrined in conventional curriculum wisdom. For another perspective see 201.

387 WALKER, R., 'Getting involved in curriculum research: a personal history', in LAWN, M. and BARTON, L. (Eds.) (337), pp. 193–213

An account of the author's involvement in curriculum research over a decade. Includes some interesting comments on SAFARI's approach to research (377). An illustration of the autobiographical trend currently in vogue within curriculum studies.

388 WARING, M., *Social Pressures and Curriculum Innovation*, Methuen, 1979

A case-study of the Nuffield O-Level Chemistry Project based on much hitherto unpublished material. Valuable chapters on 'Background to the Nuffield Foundation Science Teaching Project', 'Coordination, communication and dissemination' and 'Changing the curriculum', especially the section 'Curriculum projects and the art of the possible'.

389 WESTON, P., *Framework for the Curriculum: A Study in Secondary Schooling*, NFER, 1977

See 259.

390 WISE, R., 'The need for retrospective accounts of curriculum development', *J. Curriculum Studies*, 11:1, 1979, pp. 17–28

Argues the need for accounts by curriculum development workers of the processes of deliberation involved in the production of curriculum proposals and materials. Article asks 'us to apply the deliberative skills we use within curriculum development to our professional discussions about curriculum development'.

10 'Official' Curriculum Publications

391 DEPARTMENT of EDUCATION and SCIENCE, *A Language for Life*, (The Bullock Report), HMSO, 1975
Report of a Government Committee of Enquiry into all aspects of teaching the uses of English. A wide ranging enquiry surveying practice and thinking and making recommendations. Among the latter were proposals for introducing a national system of monitoring of pupils' performance and for school-based policies of language across the curriculum.

392 DEPARTMENT of EDUCATION and SCIENCE/WELSH OFFICE, *A New Partnership for Our Schools*, (The Taylor Report), HMSO, 1977
A report of a Committee of Enquiry into arrangements for the managing and governing of schools in England and Wales. Recommends modifications to the membership and functions of governing bodies. In relation to the curriculum, 'The governing body should be given by the local education authority the responsibility for setting the aims of the school, for considering the means by which they are pursued, for keeping under review the school's progress towards them, and for deciding upon action to facilitate such progress.'

393 DEPARTMENT of EDUCATION and SCIENCE, *Curriculum 11-16*, HMSO, 1977
A contribution by HMI to debate about the secondary school curriculum. An initial paper addresses three major themes: (a) the case for a common secondary curriculum to 16, (b) schools and society, (c) school and preparation for work. This is followed by supplementary papers on curricular areas supporting or extending the arguments in the initial paper. Argues that 'a curriculum, worked out in the ways suggested, would help to ameliorate the inconsistencies and irrationalities which at present exist, without entailing any kind of centralised control'. For a critique see 279.

394 DEPARTMENT of EDUCATION and SCIENCE/WELSH OFFICE, *Education in Schools: A Consultative Document*, HMSO, 1977

The DES summary of conclusions reached following 'The Great Debate' of 1976-77. Argues for more attention to be given to evaluation, assessment and teacher competence. States that the Secretaries of State (for Education and Wales) will 'seek to establish a broad agreement with their partners in the education service on a framework for the curriculum'.

395 DEPARTMENT of EDUCATION and SCIENCE, *Primary Education in England: A Survey by HM Inspectors of Schools*, HMSO, 1978

The results of a survey of over 1100 primary classes in England conducted between 1975 and 1977. The first, publicly accessible professional evaluation of primary education since its establishment.

396 DEPARTMENT of EDUCATION and SCIENCE, *Aspects of Secondary Education in England: A Survey by HM Inspectors of Schools*, HMSO, 1979

Report of an HMI survey into the fourth and fifth years of secondary education conducted between 1975 and 1978. It concentrates on language, mathematics, science, and personal and social development.

397 DES, *Local Authority Arrangements for the School Curriculum*, HMSO, 1979

See 256.

398 DEPARTMENT of EDUCATION and SCIENCE/WELSH OFFICE, *A Framework for the School Curriculum*, HMSO, 1980

Central government's first attempt (in recent times) to provide a curriculum framework for primary and secondary education. The framework is couched in terms of general aims, subjects, and, in some cases, allocations of time.

399 DEPARTMENT of EDUCATION and SCIENCE, *A View of the Curriculum*, HMI Series: Matters for Discussion 11, HMSO, 1980

Sets out HM Inspectorate's views of a possible curriculum for primary and secondary schools. The paper argues for a broad curriculum for all pupils up to the age of 16. 'It also seeks greater coherence and continuity in school education as a whole'.

400 DEPARTMENT of EDUCATION and SCIENCE/WELSH OFFICE, *The School Curriculum*, HMSO, 1981

The successor to *A Framework for the School Curriculum* (398). Sets out government policy in relation to the school curriculum in England and Wales. Has sections on 'Educational Aims', 'Resources', 'The Primary Phase' and 'The Secondary Phase'. Stresses that 'Neither the Government nor the local authorities should specify in detail what the schools should teach.'

401 DEPARTMENT of EDUCATION and SCIENCE, *Education 5 to 9: An Illustrative Survey of 80 First Schools in England*, HMSO, 1982

Discusses the curriculum and teaching arrangements in a sample of first schools covering the age-ranges 5 to 8 and 5 to 9.

402 DEPARTMENT of EDUCATION and SCIENCE, *Mathematics Counts*, (The Cockcroft Report), HMSO, 1982

Report of a Government Committee of Inquiry who considered the teaching of mathematics in primary and secondary schools in England and Wales. Discusses mathematics in schools, preservice and inservice training, and the mathematical needs of adult life, employment, and further and higher education.

11 Curriculum Journals

Many academic journals publish articles on aspects of curriculum studies from time to time. In addition, there are many journals concerned with the teaching of particular subjects or areas of the curriculum. The journals listed below are devoted entirely to curriculum studies or aspects of it.

403 *Curriculum*

The journal of the Association for the Study of the Curriculum. A British journal publishing articles from educationists and practising teachers on all aspects of curriculum studies and practice. Published twice a year and available from Nafferton Books, Driffield.

404 *Curriculum Inquiry*

Publishes contributions related to curriculum development, evaluation and theory. Contains major articles, extended critical reviews, and 'dialogues' between authors of papers and readers. Very largely American in orientation. Published quarterly and available from J. Wiley and Sons Ltd., 605 Third Avenue, New York, 10158.

405 *Curriculum Perspectives*

Publishes material on curriculum development, evaluation and theory. Has sections devoted to major articles, case studies and book reviews. Contributions are largely Australian. Published twice a year and available from Curriculum Perspectives, Western Australia College of Advanced Education, Churchlands Campus, Pearson Street, Churchlands, Western Australia 6153

406 *Journal of Curriculum Studies*

An international journal with editors in the United Kingdom, United States, Canada and Australia. Publishes contributions to curriculum theory, planning, evaluation, innovation and practice. Contains major articles, case studies, reports and reviews. Published quarterly and available from Taylor and Francis Ltd., 4 John Street, London WC1N 2ET

407 *Studies in Educational Evaluation*

An international journal publishing empirical evaluation studies, brief abstracts of such studies, and reflections on issues involving the evaluation of curricula. Available from Pergamon Press Ltd., Headington Hill Hall, Oxford OX3 OBW

408 *The Journal of Curriculum Theorizing*

Invites material concerned with curriculum theory, history and criticism. Especially concerned with publishing articles from reconceptualists. Almost entirely American in orientation. Published twice a year and available from the Journal of Curriculum Theorising, University of Rochester, Graduate School of Education and Human Development, Centre for the Study of Curriculum and Teaching, Rochester, New York State 14627

12 Addendum

409 AHIER, J. AND FLUDE, M. (EDS.), *Contemporary Education Policy*, Croom Helm, 1983

Argues for 'a more policy-orientated and politically aware sociology of education'. Particularly useful papers by Dale ('Thatcherism and Education') and Whitty ('State policy and school examinations 1976–82').

410 BARNES, D., *Practical Curriculum Study*, Routledge and Kegan Paul, 1982

An introduction to major curriculum themes — course-planning, the content of the curriculum, analyzing and evaluating the curriculum, and the control of the curriculum — through an explanatory text and a series of practical tasks.

411 BUSH, T. and KOGAN, M., *Directors of Education*, Allen and Unwin, 1982

A study of the role of directors of education based on interviews with four directors and an analysis of questionnaire data from 61 others. In particular, changes in the role of the director over the last ten years are explored.

412 ELLIOTT, G. (Ed.), *The School Curriculum in the 1980s*, Aspects of Education, 26, University of Hull, 1981

A 'curates-egg' collection with an interesting piece by Golby (on primary education) and useful ones by Holley (on secondary schools) and Brown (on the implementation of curriculum change by schools).

413 HORTON, T. and RAGGATT, P. (Eds.), *Challenge and Change in the Curriculum*, Hodder and Stoughton/Open University, 1982

A collection of papers examining 'questions about the role of formal education in a social and cultural context, the translation of values into guidelines and frameworks for practical implementation, and problems associated with change and renewal in the curriculum'. Contains a number of interesting papers e.g. 'Core Curriculum for Australian Schools' (Canberra Curriculum Development Centre)

414 LEE, V. and ZELDIN, D. (Eds.), *Planning in the Curriculum*, Hodder and Stoughton/Open University, 1982

A useful collection of papers dealing with curriculum planning at the institutional and the classroom levels. Editorial material is rather too brief but the book contains some interesting, not easily accessible papers including Kreiner's 'Ideology and management in a garbage can situation'!

415 MEIGHAN, R. and REID, W., 'How will the "new technology" change the curriculum?', *J. Curriculum Studies*, 14:4, 1982, pp. 353–358

A fascinating, insightful set of speculations about the roles of the home and the school in education in societies characterized by the 'new technology'.

416 NICOLL, J., *Patterns of Project Dissemination*, Schools Council Publications, 1982

Based on an analysis of the dissemination policies and procedures of 82 Schools Council projects. Discusses the funding of dissemination, publication and dissemination, main patterns of dissemination (six in all) and implications for disseminators.

417 NUTTALL, D. (Ed.), *Assessing Educational Achievement*, *Educational Analysis*, 4:2, 1982

A valuable, well-written collection of papers dealing with (a) the assessment of the individual; (b) the use of individual assessment as a means of assessing the performance of individual institutions or the education system as a whole; and (c) problematic conceptual issues in the field of educational assessment.

418 SKILBECK, M., *A Core Curriculum for the Common School*, University of London Institute of Education, 1982

An important paper considering the evolution of a nationally determined curriculum framework and putting forward a persuasive case for a core curriculum for the common school. The notion of core is examined in relation to areas of knowledge and experience, learning processes and learning environments.'

419 WINKLEY, D., 'LEA inspectors and advisers: a developmental analysis', *Oxford Review of Education*, 8:2, 1982, pp. 121–137

An indepth analysis of the past and present roles of advisers and inspectors. Includes a valuable discussion of current dilemmas — those of 'structures', 'roles and powers' and 'personal philosophies'.

Author and Editor Index

Adelman, C., 210, 354, 365
Ahier, J., 409
Anderson, D., 260
Apple, M., 32, 33, 34, 35
Ashton, P., 261, 355
Atkin, M., 36, 145, 262
Ausubel, D., 166
Ball, S., 90
Banks, J., 200
Bantock, G., 76, 77, 78
Barnes, D., 356, 357, 410
Barrow, R., 123
Barton, L., 337
Beauchamp. G., 328
Becher, T., 175, 263, 264
Beckett, L., 250
Bell, R., 101, 113
Benjamin, H., 79
Beresford, C., 114
Berlak, A., 358
Berlak, H., 358
Berman, P., 228
Bernbaum, G., 37
Bernstein, B., 38
Blackie, J., 102
Bloom, B., 146, 155, 265
Bloomer, M., 251
Blyth, W., 147
Bolam, R., 115, 116, 176
Bourdieu, P., 39
Boyd-Barrett, O., 40
Briault, E., 252
Broadfoot, P., 266
Broudy, H., 124, 359
Brown, S., 177, 229
Brownell, A., 130
Bruner, J., 125, 167
Burstall, C., 360

Bush, T., 253, 411
Bynner, J., 361
Byrne Hill, G., 41
Centre for Contemporary Cultural
   Studies, 42
C.E.R.I., 103, 117, 118, 178, 179,
   207, 208
Chanan, G., 80, 81
Cheverst, W., 362
Choppin, B., 267
Cooper, K., 230
Cronbach, L., 268
Dale, R., 43, 44
Dale, S., 27
Dalin, P., 180
Daunt, P., 254
Davie, G., 91
Davies, I., 45
Davies, I., 148, 149
Davies, W., 46
Dawson, P., 255
Dearden, R., 126, 269
Dennison, W., 270
D.E.S., 256, 391-402
Dickinson, N., 119
Dockrell, W., 363
Donaldson, M., 168
Doyle, W., 231
Durkheim, E., 92
Egan, K., 329, 330
Eggleston S.J., 47, 209
Eicholz, G., 232
Eisner, E., 10, 127, 150, 151, 152,
   201, 271, 272, 331
Elliott, G., 412
Elliott, J., 210, 233, 273, 274, 364,
   365
Eraut, M., 275, 276

Evans, P., 211
Finch, A., 13
Floyd, A., 169, 170
Flude, M., 409
Fowler, G., 48
Fullan, M., 234, 235, 236
Gagné, R., 171
Galton, M., 14
Gammage, P., 172
Gibbons, M., 95
Gibson, R., 277
Gilchrist, G., 120
Gilchrist, L., 81
Giroux, H., 49
Glatter, R., 121
Golby M., 15, 82, 332
Goldstein, H., 278
Goodlad, J., 11, 212, 237
Goodson, I., 93, 213
Gordon, P., 94
Grace, G., 50
Gray, H., 214
Green, A., 68
Greenwald, J., 172
Greig, G., 202
Gribble, J., 153
Groarke, M., 211
Gross, N., 366
Grumet, M., 333, 343, 344
Halpin, D., 279, 280
Hamilton, D., 95, 281, 282, 301, 363
Harding, J., 181, 238
Hargreaves, A., 215
Harlen, W., 182, 283, 284, 285, 286
Harnischfeger, A., 173
Harris, A., 16
Hartnett, A., 28
Hastings, J., 265
Havelock, R., 183
Hegarty, E., 367
Henderson, E., 216
Hirst, P., 218
Hogben, D., 154
Holley, B., 383
Holly, D., 184
Holt, M., 185, 217, 218, 287, 368
Hooper, R., 17
Horton, T., 413

House, E., 186, 187, 288
Hoyle, E., 219, 220
Huebner, D., 51
Hurman, A., 257, 370
Inglis, F., 129
Jackson, P., 369
Jenkins, D., 2, 289, 290, 334, 335
Johnson, M., 197, 336
Kaufman, B., 52
Keith, P., 380
Kelly, P., 181, 239, 243
Kelly, V., 3, 53
Kemmis, S., 291
Kerr. J., 4
King, A., 130
King, E., 188
Kirst, M., 54
Klein, F., 237
Kliebard, H., 96
Kogan, M., 55, 56, 57, 104, 411
Krathwohl, D., 155
Lacey, C., 292
Lawn, M., 337
Lawton, D., 5, 58, 59, 94, 292
Layton, D., 97
Lee, V., 414
Lello, J., 293
Lortie, D., 60
MacDonald, B., 189, 226, 240, 294, 295, 371
MacDonald, G., 105
MacDonald, J., 61
MacDonald, M., 62
MacDonald-Ross, M., 156
MacIntosh, H., 296
McCormick, R., 297, 298
McIntyre, D., 177, 299
McLanghlin, W., 228
MacLure, S., 63, 175, 190, 263
Madaus, G., 265
Mager, R., 157
Marsden, W., 98
Meigham, R., 415
Middleton, D., 372
Miles, M., 221
Morris, K., 29
Munroe, R., 300
Musgrove, F., 64

Nicodemus, R., 181
Nicoll, J., 416
Nisbet, J., 191
Nixon, J., 373
Nuttall, O., 417
Nyquist, E., 192
O'Keefe, D., 338
Olson, J., 374, 375
Oram, R., 339
Owen, J., 193
Packwood, T., 104
Parker, J., 131
Parlett, M., 301
Parsons, C., 245, 246, 302, 303
Perry, G., 216
Phenix, P., 132
Pidgeon, D., 327
Pinar, W., 340, 341, 342, 343, 344
Pomfret, A., 236
Ponder, G., 231
Popham, W., 158
Pratt, D., 133, 159
Prescott, W., 101, 106, 222
Pring, R., 65, 134, 160, 304
Raggatt, P., 413
Raths, J., 161
Redknap, C., 122
Reedy, S., 18
Reid, W., 194, 202, 345, 346, 376, 383, 415
Reynolds, J., 83, 162
Richards, C., 9, 19, 20, 21, 107, 384
Rogers, E., 232
Rowntree, D., 135
Rubin, L., 22, 131
Rudduck, J., 240, 241, 242, 243
SAFARI, 377
Salter, B., 66, 245, 246
Sarason, S., 223
Satterley, D., 305
Schon, D., 195
Schools Council, 136, 203, 244, 306
Schubert, W., 30
Schwab, J., 347, 348, 349
Scrimshaw, P., 13, 67, 307
Scriven, M., 308, 309
Seguel, M., 99
Sharp, R., 68

Shaw, K., 251, 350, 378
Shipman, M., 2, 204, 205, 310, 379
Shores, J., 7
Sieber, S., 196
Simon, B., 351, 352
Simons, H., 290, 311
Skilbeck, M., 6, 83, 84, 85, 137, 162, 224, 418
Smetherham, D., 312
Smith, B., 7
Smith, F., 252
Smith, L., 380
Sockett, H., 138, 139, 140, 141, 163, 313, 314
Soulsby, D., 174
Stake, R., 315, 316
Stanley, W., 7
Steadman, S., 245, 246, 317
Stenhouse, L., 12, 23, 86, 142, 164, 165, 318, 319, 320, 381, 382
Straughan, R., 321
Taba, H., 8
Tapper, T., 66
Tawney, D., 322
Taylor, P., 9, 24, 25, 26, 197, 225, 383, 384
Taylor, W., 198
Trenaman, N., 108
Tye, K., 26
Tyler, L., 31
Tyler, R., 143, 323
Vallance, E., 127
Walker, D., 54, 194, 206, 385, 386
Walker, R., 186, 226, 290, 371, 387
Walton, J., 25, 227, 258
Waring, M., 109, 247, 388
Warnock, M., 87
Watson, F., 100
Watson, G., 248
Webster, J., 199
Welton, J., 227
Westbury, I., 353
Weston, P., 259, 389
White, J., 88, 89, 110, 324
Whitehead, D., 249
Whiteside, T., 69
Whitfield, R., 144
Whitty, G., 70, 71, 72

Wiley, D., 173
Wilkof, N., 353
Williams, R., 73
Willis, G., 325, 326
Winkley, O., 419
Wise, A., 390
Wiseman, S., 327

Woodhead, M., 18
Wrigley, J., 321
Wyatt, T., 111
Young, M., 72, 74, 75
Zaret, E., 61
Zeldin, D., 414

THE ASSOCIATION FOR THE STUDY OF THE CURRICULUM

Users of this bibilography who find curriculum studies of interest are recommended to join the Association for the Study of the Curriculum. This was created in 1977 from the Standing Conference on Curriculum Studies which had met each year since 1973. The purpose of the association is to bring together people working in different educational contexts in a creative discussion of curriculum issues. The association holds an annual conference, publishes material and has a growing number of associated local groups. Membership is open to anyone concerned with curriculum study and/or its practical implementation in a school, university, college, national or local institution, and to other people who are specially interested in or have worked notably in the field of curriculum.

For Product Safety Concerns and Information please contact our EU
representative GPSR@taylorandfrancis.com
Taylor & Francis Verlag GmbH, Kaufingerstraße 24, 80331 München, Germany

www.ingramcontent.com/pod-product-compliance
Lightning Source LLC
Chambersburg PA
CBHW051759230426
43670CB00012B/2348